10

MINUTE GUIDE TO

WORKING WITH FINANCIAL ADVISORS

by Barbara Hetzer

alpha
books

Macmillan Spectrum/Alpha Books

A Division of Macmillan General Reference
A Simon & Schuster Macmillan Company
1633 Broadway, New York, NY 10019-6705

12-98   # 36955585

International Standard Book Number: 0-02-861548-4
Library of Congress Catalog Card Number: 96-078162

99 98 97   8   7   6   5   4   3   2   1

Interpretation of the printing code: the rightmost double-digit number is the year of the book's first printing; the rightmost single-digit number is the number of the book's printing. For example, a printing code of 97-1 shows that this copy of the book was printed during the first printing of the book in 1997.

Printed in the United States of America

Publisher: Theresa Murtha

Editor in Chief: Richard J. Staron

Production Editor: Michael Thomas

Copy Editors: Chris Van Camp, Michael Thomas

Cover Designer: Dan Armstrong

Designer: Glenn Larsen

Indexer: Nadia Ibrahim

Production Team: Angela Calvert, Kim Cofer, Diana Groth, Maureen Hanrahan, Malinda Kuhn, Christy Wagner

CONTENTS

INTRODUCTION

Finding good professional help isn't easy. No matter what your dilemma, you'll find an assortment of advisors just waiting to win you as a client. Some of them offer impeccable service. Others are okay in a pinch. A handful are downright unscrupulous. You'll find many advisors employed by firms—some new and some established—some with international representation, some with regional coverage, and other advisors working in one- or two-person shops. As more and more professionals lose their jobs to corporate downsizing, in fact, every Tom, Dick, and Harriet seems to be hanging out a shingle, professing their expertise in one field or another.

What makes picking an advisor so tricky, however, is not just the vast number of choices available but the fact that you must find someone who is trustworthy, eager to protect your interests, and—for most of you—reasonably priced. Also, you may not want to admit that you can't do it yourself, or that you dread confiding the not-frequently-talked-about details of your life to a virtual stranger.

So what are you going to do? Occasionally, you *will* need to seek expert counsel. It's inevitable, no matter how well you manage your budget and the rest of your financial affairs. At some point, you'll want to borrow money to buy a house. (You can't arrange for a mortgage without the help of a broker or banker.) Or you'll have a car accident. (You'll need to deal with your insurance agent.)

Being prepared, however, always makes the process of finding and working with a professional advisor that much easier. And with the help of this book, you'll learn everything you need to know about working with a lawyer, a certified public accountant, a stockbroker, and other financial advisors.

If you're faced with a specific problem right now, by all means head straight for those lessons that address the issue at hand. Otherwise, start from the beginning, as you would any other book. You'll learn the difference between a professional hawking "accounting services" and a certified public accountant. You'll learn the difference between a buyer's real estate agent and a seller's real estate agent. You'll learn which advisors charge by the hour, and which charge per project.

You'll learn which professions are licensed and monitored regularly for wrongdoing, and which professions are more casually defined or regulated. You'll learn which credentials to look for, which professional organizations to check out, and what some *really good* questions to ask are. Finally, you'll learn about some low-cost alternatives to traditional services, and when it's really a waste of time and money to consult a professional advisor.

CONVENTIONS USED IN THIS BOOK

You'll find the following icons used throughout this book to help you understand technical terms and to highlight hidden dangers and helpful shortcuts:

tip **Timesaver Tip** icons offer ideas that save time and eliminate confusion.

  Plain English icons define new and complicated terms.

> **!** **Panic Button** icons identify potential problems and how to solve them.

Acknowledgments

Warmest thanks to all who contributed to the research needed for this book, especially Donald Henig of the Mortgage Tech Group, Jayna Neagle of the Insurance Information Institute, Fritz Elmendorf of the Consumer Banking Association, Sona Pincholy, Michael Hetzer, Tony Cassino, Beanna Whitlock, the American Bar Association, Mary Ellen Spiegel of Fiscal Plus, Andrew Blackman of Shapiro & Lobel, James Shambo of Lifetime Planning Concepts—and to my mother, who kept the kids entertained while I was writing.

The Author

Barbara Hetzer is a journalist who writes frequently about business and personal finance issues. Her work has appeared in numerous publications, including *Business Week*, *Advertising Age*, *Fortune*, *Self*, *Working Mother*, *Business Month*, *First for Women*, and *Cosmopolitan*.

WHO'S OUT THERE?

In this lesson, you will learn what a financial advisor can do for you, and when it's best to use such counsel.

WHEN YOU NEED OUTSIDE ADVICE

Managing your personal finances can be a troublesome affair. It's often mind-numbingly complicated. Also, it's not something you're apt to casually discuss with your neighbor on the morning commuter train. It's easy to feel like you're *missing* something. If only you had an expert's opinion every now and again.

Even if you feel that you've managed your finances reasonably well thus far on your own, you have to assume that at some point you'll need some assistance. What happens when your mother, who lives halfway across the country, dies? Will a lawyer handle her estate? What can you expect him to do—and how much will it cost? Or, now that you're expecting a second child, you've started to wonder about life insurance. How much will you need, and where can you buy it?

Whether you need that occasional expert "reality check" to make sure that your finances are in line or some professional guidance to see you through a particularly prickly situation, there's a financial advisor out there, ready to assist you with every conceivable financial conundrum you might run up against.

WHAT IS A FINANCIAL ADVISOR?

Lawyers can negotiate the alimony and child-support payments in a divorce settlement. *Financial planners* will draft a retirement saving plan for you and your spouse. *Accountants* prepare your taxes. *Real estate brokers* help you get the highest price when selling your house. *Stockbrokers* give you tips on the fastest-growing stocks. All of these professionals are *financial advisors*.

 Financial Advisor A financial advisor is a professional who advises you on how to spend your money, how to save your money, and, frequently, how to make *more* money.

But no matter what these financial wizards say—or how forcefully they say it—you, the consumer, have the last word. When you hire an advisor it may sure seem like you're turning over the control of your finances. But you're not. Financial advisors don't *manage* your money. They merely offer you professional advice, which you may or may not choose to follow. Advisors will certainly offer strong recommendations and suggestions—in some cases they'll even *tell* you what to do— but they can't take any action without your consent. (If they do, that's not only unethical, but illegal.) You always have the option of saying, "Thanks, but no thanks."

Of course, this advice (about using financial advice) only applies when you're working with a reputable professional. There are some unscrupulous people out there who may urge you to "just leave everything to me." That's not advisable—under any circumstances. In each professional category that follows, you'll find a section called "the necessary credentials." Top-notch professionals have these qualifications. Borderline, quasi-professionals generally don't.

Should you find yourself in a less-than-perfect advisory situation, you may have some recourse. Especially if you have a contract (which is always a good idea) and the advisor didn't provide the agreed-upon services. You can always seek legal counsel to rectify a situation (although that's generally very costly), but you might settle matters simply by complaining to the governing body that licenses the particular profession. If you don't know who that is (it varies from one profession to another), contact your local Better Business Bureau or the profession's most prominent organization. They should be able to direct your complaint to the proper authority.

tip **Protect Yourself** One easy way to protect yourself is to make sure that you understand the services your financial advisor will be providing. They should be spelled out in a contract or similar written proposal.

You should know, in advance, roughly how much an advisor's services will cost you. Some financial advisors charge a flat fee for services rendered; others charge an hourly rate, plus an additional fee to cover out-of-pocket expenses. Other advisors charge a commission, which can fluctuate depending upon how frequently you use their services and/or what types of financial products you buy. One payment schedule isn't really better than another, as long as you know up front how much you'll be expected to fork over for your advisor's counsel.

FINDING A REPUTABLE ADVISOR

The single best way to find any type of advisor is through a personal reference. When you need a lawyer, for example, most of you will probably think to ask your sister, your neighbor, even a colleague or two, whom they've had represent them in the past. But don't stop there. Ask for references from as many people as you can who face situations similar to your own. If you need a lawyer to handle your divorce, for instance, ask the divorced parents at the next PTA meeting who they would recommend. By all means, ask other professionals that you already have a working relationship with for references, too. Your banker can probably recommend a financial planner; your accountant, a stockbroker; your real estate broker, a mortgage broker.

You can also get referrals from professional organizations, such as the American Institute of Certified Public Accountants and The National Association of Personal Financial Advisors, that operate nationwide. Being a member in good standing is no guarantee that a particular financial advisor is reliable and honest, but it's a safer bet than picking an advisor blindly from an ad in the yellow pages—especially if membership involves more than just signing up and paying an annual fee. Seek out candidates from organizations that require members to take examinations and/or continuing education classes, log a certain amount of on-the-job experience, and adhere to a code of ethics.

Once you've drawn up a list of contenders, contact each of them by phone. You'll want to meet them in person, of course, but that comes later. For now, your objective is to pare that list down to two or three very strong candidates. Over the phone, briefly do the following:

- Identify yourself and your problem.

- Explain how you were referred to the advisor.

- Find out if he is taking on new clients.

- Find out how soon he could tackle your problem.

- Ask about his credentials.

- Find out roughly how much he charges.

If you like the answers to these questions, you'll probably want to meet with the advisor in person. Most initial consultations are *free,* but don't assume yours will be. The purpose of the visit is to determine if you like the advisor himself and his method of doing business. Would you feel comfortable working with him, for instance? Do you trust him? Can you imagine telling him some of the most intimate details of your financial life? You'll have to, in many cases.

tip   **Don't Expect Any Freebies**   Although an initial consultation may be free, don't expect any freebies. You'll get little, if any, actual advice at this meeting.

SITUATIONS THAT SHOULD BE AVOIDED

You can—and should—ask an advisor about his background. If the details he gives you don't pan out under investigation—he *says* he's worked for the brokerage firm for ten years (it's been ten *months*), or he *says* he graduated from Harvard (he didn't)—drop him like a hot potato. You don't want to be bothered with such nonsense. Nor is it a good indication of how fairly he'll represent your interests in the future.

Don't be afraid to probe into his work history either. In each professional category that follows, you'll find specific suggestions about how to check up on a financial advisor. In every instance, however, you can certainly ask the advisor himself if he's ever been accused of or committed any wrongdoing. If he refuses to give you an answer—he may argue, "That's not pertinent to our working relationship," or "I never discuss such matters with new clients"—drop this guy, too. You have every right to an honest answer to this question. And now's the perfect time to discuss this matter, *before* you let him handle your affairs.

You might also want to ask an advisor for some references. Of course, you can't rely too heavily on these recommendations. An advisor's not going to suggest that you call the clients who weren't happy with his work. Still, you might glean some useful tidbits about your potential advisor if you ask his references questions such as the following:

- What did the advisor do for you specifically?
- What part of his work were you least satisfied with? Most satisfied with?
- Did he do everything that he promised?
- Why are you no longer using his services? Or, would you use his services again, if a need arose?

> **!** **No Excuses** What if the advisor refuses to give you any references, citing client confidentiality? That's a bogus excuse. Every professional can give you references. He just has to check with the clients first, before giving their names out to potential customers like you. Either your advisor is too lazy to call up a few customers to get their approval (and who wants to hire someone who's lazy?), or he doesn't have many happy, satisfied clients. In either case, drop him.

If, at that initial meeting or in subsequent meetings, an advisor seems too busy to answer your questions or gives you an incomprehensible answer (that you're too embarrassed to admit you don't understand), look for someone else. Why?

First, these advisors may hold lots of fancy degrees, and they may be a lot more knowledgeable than you about certain things, but they're still doing a job. That's what you're paying them for, in fact. Don't be shy about demanding your money's worth. Second, a good lawyer or a good insurance agent or a good tax accountant knows how to explain what he does in *plain English*. You shouldn't feel apologetic about asking. Nor should they make you feel that way. Again, you're paying for those explanations.

Finally, you need to pick a professional with a good bedside manner. If something happens—your house burns down, your spouse of 25 years just left you and is trying to keep you from getting a dime—you need someone you can trust. The crisis itself is bad enough. You don't need a professional who is tough to deal with, too.

In this lesson, you learned what a financial advisor can do for you, and when it's best to use such counsel. In the next lesson, you will learn what a financial planner can do for you, and how financial planners are compensated for their services.

WORKING WITH A FINANCIAL PLANNER—PART 1

In this lesson, you will learn what a financial planner can do for you, and how financial planners are compensated for their services.

WHO NEEDS *PROFESSIONAL* FINANCIAL PLANNING?

Whether it's a recent divorce, the birth of a child, or that long-awaited graduation from college, you'd probably benefit from some financial guidance during "life changes" that can dramatically affect your finances. Your financial objectives—not to mention your budget—are shifting, and the strategies that worked in the past may no longer meet your needs.

Perhaps you don't need a *complete* financial makeover. But you need to know if you're saving enough for your children's education. Or, you're wondering if you could possibly take your firm's early retirement package and make do on a lesser salary. Even if you've drawn up your own financial game plan and it seems to be working, it would help to get an expert opinion about whether you're taking the right steps. Financial planners can help steer you through these financial quagmires.

WHAT A FINANCIAL PLANNER CAN DO FOR YOU

A financial planner helps you manage your money better. He can advise you on a complex financial situation like setting up a trust—or simply help you budget and save better. He can devise a plan to meet a short-term financial goal, such as saving for a house, or help you plot a long-term retirement plan. He can address a single issue such as retirement planning, or develop a comprehensive plan that covers every aspect of your financial future. He can give you advice on almost any personal finance concern, including:

- Personal debt
- Budgeting
- Funding a child's college education
- Estate planning
- Taxes
- Retirement planning
- Starting your own business
- Cash flow
- Caring for an elderly parent
- Just saving for a "rainy day"

Generally, the financial planning process begins by outlining your goals, both short- and long-term. What do you want? A car? Enough money to retire comfortably, or to send your kids to an Ivy League school? A house in the country? A financial planner will ask these questions, and more, so that he can identify your objectives. He can't develop a workable plan until he's first laid out your goals.

Next, he'll want to take stock of your current financial situation. How much money did you earn last year? How much debt do you owe? Do you have any money saved or invested? A planner will typically gauge how much money you have on hand in two ways. First, he'll examine your cash flow. (That's monthly earnings minus monthly expenses. Obviously, you should have some earnings left over at the end of each month.) Second, he'll figure your net worth. (That's assets minus liabilities, or what you'd have left if you sold all your possessions and paid all your debts.)

Based on the answers to all of these questions, a financial planner will then map out a customized *financial plan*, which suggests various ways to trim your budget and to invest your money. The result? You'll pay off that Visa card, buy a 40-foot boat, retire at 60, or whatever else you wanted to do with your money.

tip   **Too Much Help?**   In many cases, clients don't want, or need, a complete financial makeover. No problem. Planners can focus on just one or two tough issues instead. You may simply want the planner to review your retirement savings plan, for instance. Are you saving enough each year? Should you put more into equities? Or you may want answers to some specific financial questions concerning your divorce settlement or current cash flow.

At this point, you may want to end the relationship with your planner. Many consumers walk away—professional plan or answer to a specific problem in hand—intending to handle any future financial questions themselves. Other people, however, want their planner to update their financial plan periodically—usually once a year, or else during a major "life change"—as their needs and goals change.

WHEN YOU *DON'T* NEED TO SEE A FINANCIAL PLANNER

Like most people, you'll probably benefit from seeking a financial planner's advice at some stage in your life. But if everything truly seems to be in order—you're saving for retirement; you don't spend more than you earn; except for your home mortgage, you're not in debt—and all you need is to make a will, buy some additional life insurance, or get out of debt, you're probably throwing your money away on a financial planner's advice. Here's why:

- Financial planners can't draft wills. (Lawyers can.)

- Although a large percentage of financial planners also sell insurance, you can buy insurance just as easily from an insurance agent—without paying a planner's fee.

- If you're over your head in debt, the last thing you want to do is to pay someone to help you figure out how to stop spending so much. Contact the National Foundation for Consumer Credit (800-388-2227) instead. One of their counselors will help you create a workable budget and repayment plan for free or for a nominal charge.

> **tip**
>
> **Low-Cost Alternative**   Money Minds (800-ASK-A-CFP) answers specific financial questions about investing or preparing your taxes—over the phone. The cost: $3.95 per minute. This independent group of certified public accountants and certified financial planners also offers more in-depth analysis, too. For a comprehensive financial plan, they charge an hourly rate (up to $125 per hour). For retirement and estate planning, they charge a percentage of the assets managed.

COMPENSATION, COMMISSION, AND OTHER FEES

There are many types of financial planners. One important distinction is how they're paid.

The *fee-only* planner is paid solely for the service rendered: his advice. He does not receive a commission for any recommended investments that you purchase.

To create your financial plan, fee-only planners charge either an hourly fee, ranging from $75 to $300 per hour, or a flat rate for the entire project, ranging from $450 to $6,000. (For complex estate plans, that figure could be as high as $10,000.) To ensure that the plan is implemented, fee-only planners often manage their client's investments as well—for an additional annual retainer of .5% to 2% of the assets managed, per year.

The *commission-only* planner doesn't charge you for his advice, or for designing your personal financial plan. Instead, he earns a commission from the mutual fund, annuity, or other investment that you purchase—at his recommendation—to put his financial plan into action. The only way that this particular planner gets paid, in fact, is when you buy the products he recommends.

The *fee-based* planner is basically a hybrid of the two. Like a fee-only planner, a fee-based planner charges a fee for his advice and your financial plan preparation. In addition, he may receive a commission—much like a commission-only planner—from investments he recommends to help you reach your financial objectives.

tip   **Suggest a Change**   If you're worried about a possible conflict of interest—and the financial planner that you've selected works on a fee-plus-commission basis—you don't have to buy the products from him. You can do that on your own. Just let the planner know from the outset that you don't want to buy any products from him. Tell him you'd rather work on a fee basis only.

The *fee-offset* planner will charge you for advice and financial plan preparation initially. But that fee may be "offset" against commissions the planner receives later when you buy recommended investments.

In many cases, the fee-offset planner's fee will be waived—or reimbursed, if you've already paid it—if the commission that he earns is more than the fee that you were charged. For instance, you won't actually have to fork over that $600 planning fee *if* you buy mutual funds from the planner that earn him a $600 commission.

> **!** **Conflict of Interest**   Consumer advocates insist
> that fee-only planning is best. Why? Since fee-only
> planners don't earn commission from the products
> that they recommend, there's no apparent conflict
> between their financial interest and yours. It's hard
> to imagine that someone who's paid to sell you a
> product—as commission-based planners are—
> can really offer objective advice.

Trouble is, of course, fee-only planners tend to charge more.
Since many have minimum fees of at least $2,000, a reputable
fee-only planner may be more than you can afford, especially
if you're a small or beginning investor. If you want help
choosing, let's say, a mutual fund to stash retirement savings,
you might do better choosing a fee-based planner. Often, fee-
based clients get load funds and the planner gets the commission in lieu of a fee.

In this lesson, you learned what a financial planner can do for
you, and how financial planners are compensated for their
services. In the next lesson, you will learn how to select a financial planner, and what some *really* good questions to ask a
planner are.

WORKING WITH A FINANCIAL PLANNER—PART 2

In this lesson, you will learn how to select a financial planner, and what some really good questions to ask a planner are.

THE NECESSARY CREDENTIALS

The term *financial planner* is basically meaningless. There's no accepted definition of *financial planner* nor are there any educational requirements. The profession is so loosely regulated, in fact, that anyone—your hairdresser, your mother-in-law, even your kid's camp counselor—can claim to be a planner, and get paid for it.

Obviously, many planners do have admirable educational and on-the-job credentials. But you can't assume that all do. A few planners are out-and-out frauds. Others offer self-serving advice. And some are merely incompetent. To separate the good from the bad, look for the following credentials and designations:

- *Certified Financial Planner (CFP).* A certified financial planner must complete a two-year program in tax planning, investments, and other aspects of personal finance (such training is conducted by the highly respected College for Financial Planning in Denver, Colorado), and then pass a ten-hour exam. Some three years' work experience is also required before the Certified Financial Planning Board of Standards will award a license. CFPs adhere to a professional code of ethics and log roughly 30 hours of continuing education every two years in their field of specialization.

- *Chartered Financial Consultant (CFC)*. A chartered financial consultant must pass 10 college-level courses in financial planning, wealth accumulation, and estate planning at the American College in Bryn Mawr, Pennsylvania. CFCs must have at least three years of practical industry experience. Continuing education is also required.

- *Personal Financial Specialist (PFS)*. A personal financial specialist is a certified public accountant who's trained in personal finance. This designation, given by the American Institute of Certified Public Accountants, is granted to CPAs who've passed a 6-hour test and have had at least three years' experience in financial planning. Continuing education is a must.

Obviously, these designations aren't seals of approval. But at least you're assured the planner has received some basic training before he or she hangs out a shingle. You could also check with the Securities and Exchange Commission (SEC). Anyone who is paid to give out investment advice is required to file an application with the SEC and pay a one-time fee of $150 as a *registered investment advisor*. No education or work experience is required for this designation, however.

In every state except Colorado, Iowa, Ohio, and Wyoming, planners generally must file with their state securities department. Again, this doesn't exactly grant governmental approval, but it's somewhat comforting to know your planner isn't some fly-by-nighter who hasn't even bothered to fill out the necessary forms.

> ***tip*** **Look for Benchmarks** It's probably best to choose a planner who has one of the above designations *plus* a college degree in accounting, marketing, economics, business administration, or finance, and at least three to five years of relevant work experience.

FINDING A PLANNER

The best place to find any professional is through a personal reference. Ask your lawyer, doctor, or accountant, even your friends and relatives, for the names of financial planners whose services they themselves have used. If that search doesn't turn up any good candidates, contact the consumer assistance lines at the following organizations for referrals in your area:

- The Institute of Certified Financial Planners (ICFP)
  3801 E. Florida Avenue, Suite 708
  Denver, Colorado 80210-2571
  tel.: 800-282-7526

- The International Association for Financial Planning
     (IAFP)
  5775 Glenridge Drive N.E., Suite B-300
  Atlanta, Georgia 30328
  tel.: 800-945-4237

- The National Association of Personal Financial
     Advisors (NAPFA)
   355 West Dundee Road, Suite 107
   Buffalo Grove, Illinois, 60089
   tel.: 800-FEE-ONLY

- American Society of CLU & ChFC
   270 South Bryn Mawr Avenue
   Bryn Mawr, Pennsylvania 19010-2195
   tel.: 800-392-6900

- The American Institute of Certified Public
     Accountants (AICPA)
   1211 Avenue of the Americas
   New York, New York, 10036
   tel.: 800-862-4272

Once you've found some potential candidates, conduct a brief phone interview with each. Be sure to ask these questions:

- What services do you provide?

- How long have you been in business?

- How are you paid?

The answers to these questions should help narrow down your choices. If you need help saving for your kid's college education, and two of the planners that you spoke with deal mainly with estate planning, cross them off the list.

Try to meet with your top two or three choices *in person*. Usually, there's no charge for an initial visit with a planner. It's more like a let's-get-acquainted session. You want to know if you like his or her business philosophy and personality. If he's too aggressive—and that makes you uncomfortable—look for another candidate. He, meanwhile, should be asking you questions to determine whether he can handle your specific problems.

Assuming you're satisfied with the planner after your first meeting, your should then check out the planner's disciplinary record. Are there any complaints or legal actions pending against your potential candidate? The Better Business Bureau and your state securities regulator should be able to give you that information. If the planner is a CFP, the Certified Financial Planner Board of Standards (1660 Lincoln Street, Suite 3050, Denver, Colorado 80264; tel.: 888-CFP-MARK) can tell you if the planner has ever been disciplined for ethical or legal violations.

One of the best sources of information about a planner's history, qualifications, and possible conflicts of interest, however, is a document called Form ADV. Most planners are required to file this form with federal regulators and their state securities department. They're also required to give *you* Part II (or a brochure that answers the same questions).

Don't settle for that, though. Ask for Part I of Form ADV, too. Planners aren't required to give this to you, but most will, when asked. It discloses any legal or financial difficulties that the planner has had. And it discloses any disciplinary action that regulators may have taken against the planner.

! **Check Their Business History**   Find out how long the planner has been in business, especially in your area. Less reputable practitioners often move from city to city. Longevity generally indicates a certain level of competency. If the planner you're thinking about hiring has moved around frequently, you'd better think twice about hiring him.

Eleven *Really* Good Questions to Ask a Financial Planner

Before you retain a financial planner's services, ask him or her the following questions:

1. *What's your background?* Feel free to grill him about his education, professional affiliations, and business history.

2. *What areas do you specialize in?* All planners know something about retirement planning, but if that's your main concern, make sure you find a planner who specializes in it.

3. *Who's your average client?* Many planners work primarily with a certain type of client, specializing in a particular profession, income level, or age group. The net worth and income level of the planner's average client should mirror your own.

4. *How do you prepare a plan?* Ask to see a sample plan.

5. *What should I expect?* Find out how much written advice you'll get and the number of expected meetings.

6. *Will there be any follow-up consultations once the plan is prepared and implemented?* Usually, there's an additional charge. Find out how much it is.

7. *Do you receive commissions for the products that you recommend?* If the planner receives commissions, he should tell you so *now*, and provide you with a list of products and the commissions offered.

8. *How much do you charge?* The planner should be able to give you a ballpark figure. In general, a financial plan ranges from $250 for a basic plan to $4,000 and up for a complex one.

9. *Have you ever been suspended or reprimanded for your business practices?* If he's not up front about this issue now, you most likely can break even a signed agreement should you learn later on that he wasn't telling the truth.

10. *Whom may I call as a reference?* You want to talk with people who have been clients of the planner for at least three years, and who are in a financial situation similar to yours—i.e., the planner managed their retirement accounts and that's what you want him to do for you. Ask the clients: Did you get your money's worth? How soon did he return calls? Did the planner do what he said he would?

11. *How accessible are you?* You'll have to answer this question yourself. Does he explain strategies, types of investments, and other terms clearly? Or does he merely rattle off a lot of jargon about yields, dollar cost averaging, and asset allocation, expecting you to follow along? Remember: You're paying for this service. He should speak in a language that you understand.

! Takes the Fifth   If a planner refuses to answer any or all of these questions, look elsewhere. Immediately.

Once you find a planner who answers these questions to your satisfaction, and you've checked out his references, ask for a service agreement, or an engagement letter. It spells out the services to be rendered and the corresponding charges. Like most service agreements, this will prevent confusion later on.

At no point during the financial planning process—whether it's during the initial stages of the relationship or not—should you be afraid to ask questions. If you're confused about a particular investment choice or strategy, ask the planner. Take time to think about the planner's recommendations before acting upon them. And never do or sign anything that you don't understand.

In this lesson, you learned how to select a financial planner, and what some *really* good questions to ask a planner are. In the next lesson, you will learn what a CPA can do for you.

WORKING WITH A CERTIFIED PUBLIC ACCOUNTANT

In this lesson, you will learn what a certified public accountant can do for you.

CPAS ARE NOT JUST FOR THE RICH AND FAMOUS

Mention that you're working with a certified public accountant (or CPA, as most people refer to them) and your friends will think you've struck it rich. The general public assumes, erroneously, that a CPA's job is to audit the financial statements of large corporations like General Motors and IBM, or very wealthy individuals such as the Rockefellers or the Kennedys.

While certain CPAs *do* perform those functions, many CPAs can be of service to the average consumer like you. They can prepare your tax returns, recommend tax planning strategies, even provide personal financial planning advice. Most important, they can advise you if you're being audited by the Internal Revenue Service.

Certified Public Accountant (CPA)   A CPA is a financial advisor who inspects (or *audits*) the financial records of individuals and businesses. He also prepares tax returns and gives advice on financial and tax-related matters. Unlike an "accountant," a CPA is licensed by the state.

WHO NEEDS A CPA—AND WHAT CAN HE OR SHE DO FOR YOU?

You need a CPA if your tax return is complex. (Obviously, if you file a non-itemized return like the 1040EZ, and can do it yourself, you *don't* have a complicated return.) Perhaps you're self-employed. That means you're eligible for a host of deductions—but which ones, and how much? Too many deductions, in fact, can trigger an audit by the IRS. Perhaps you live in Hoboken, New Jersey, but work just across the river in New York City, *another state*. Do you realize that you have to pay non-resident's tax on the money you earn? Do you know how much?

Even if you earn a standard salary with no bonus or other additional compensation, your tax return could be complicated by things that you own. Can you deduct your little bungalow by the sea as a rental property, for instance, if you rent it out for the winter months but you live there during July and August? Perhaps you have some stock holdings. If they've appreciated substantially over the years, how much tax will you owe when you cash them in this year? These are all questions that a CPA can address when preparing your tax return.

But that's not all. A CPA can also look at your tax picture *long term.* He'll explain how certain decisions like selling that appreciated stock or accepting a lump-sum retirement package will affect your tax situation over time. Often, he'll then recommend a tax planning strategy to implement over the next year, or several years, which could save you thousands of dollars in taxes.

tip   **"Certified"**   What can CPAs do that no other financial advisor can? They can examine the financial statements of a business and deliver a "certified audit." Consumers hardly ever need such a service, however.

In addition, CPAs can represent you, the taxpayer, before the IRS, should you be called in for an audit. A CPA will advise you on how to proceed, and whether he thinks the IRS's inquiry is routine or not. He'll even accompany you to your meeting with the IRS—or, if you grant him a power of attorney, he'll talk to the IRS without you.

Aside from taxes, a CPA can also advise you about personal financial planning. Like most other financial planners, a CPA can offer guidance on just one aspect of your finances, such as building college funds for your newborn, or he can help you develop a comprehensive financial plan.

Like most financial planners, a CPA can go beyond just developing a personal financial plan. He can monitor your plan, proposing changes as your needs and circumstances change, and assist you with putting the plan into action as well. Since most CPAs have a solid background in tax law, however, they might be able to offer some advice on tax liability (resulting from estate planning, let's say) and ways to minimize or defer that liability that a regular financial planner might not.

> **!** **Not Stock Pickers**   The CPA who also does financial planning is often weakest in the investment area. He may suggest that you invest in a mutual fund, for instance, but he won't recommend a particular fund by name.

The Necessary Credentials

Certified public accountants are licensed by the state. Just plain "accountants" are not. Most states require a CPA candidate to have at least a college degree or its equivalent, although some states now require post-graduate work, too.

To get licensed in most states—and to earn the right to list those three little letters (CPA) after his name—a CPA candidate must work under a CPA's supervision for two years and pass a uniform, national examination that tests him in accountancy, taxation, and business law. (The test takes two and one-half days to complete.) Most states also require CPAs to take some amount of continuing education courses.

> **!** **Accounting Services**   In many states you can't advertise as an *accountant* unless you're actually a certified public accountant. Non-CPAs get around this rule by marketing themselves under the terms "accounting services," "bookkeeping," or "tax preparation." It's perfectly legal, if somewhat misleading to the public.

Over 310,000 CPAs belong to the American Institute of Certified Public Accountants (AICPA), the most prominent professional organization of CPAs. Although membership doesn't actually guarantee ethical or top-notch service, members must meet extensive continuing education requirements and must abide by a code of ethics to remain members in good standing.

Some CPAs also list the certified financial planner (CFP) designation after their name and CPA title, too. (See Lesson 3 for an explanation of this designation.) Others use PFS instead, which stands for Personal Financial Specialist, an accreditation that is granted exclusively to CPAs who are members of the AICPA. To become a PFS, a CPA must log at least 250 hours per year, for three years, in some area of personal financial planning such as estate planning or retirement planning. He must then pass a six-hour exam on various financial planning issues.

FINDING A CPA

To find a reputable CPA, your best bet is to get a personal referral. Ideally, you should ask for references from people who have financial situations and/or problems similar to yours.

If you can't find a CPA through the grapevine, call your state CPA society. Often, the group will send you a list of CPAs in your area. You can also contact the American Institute of Certified Public Accountants for a list of the Personal Financial Specialists in your area. Call the AICPA at 800-862-4272; select menu #1 for the order department; and request product # GOO616.

tip **Big Six** You may have heard about accountants who work for the "Big Six." These are the largest (and most prestigious) public accounting firms in the country. Unfortunately, these *are* the guys who crunch numbers for General Motors, IBM, and other corporations. They don't handle individual tax returns. (At least not for the *average* consumer.)

Once you've found a CPA, call the state board of public accountancy to make sure that the CPA is licensed to practice in your state. You can also check with them to see if any disciplinary actions have been taken against the CPA. (If you're not happy with the quality of the CPA's service, you can file a formal complaint here, too, with the board's office of professional discipline, which will then investigate the matter. Generally, your complaint must be in writing.)

SIX *REALLY* GOOD QUESTIONS TO ASK YOUR CPA

Here is a list of questions to ask your CPA:

1. *Have you helped a client in a situation similar to mine?* It saves time to work with an accountant who knows exactly how to deal with problems like yours.

2. *What can I do to help?* A good deal of the CPA's time can be saved—and your expense lessened—if you prepare some information beforehand. Start by keeping good records.

3. *How long have you been providing accounting services and in what areas do you specialize, if any?* Professional

services don't come with guarantees. But years of
relevant experience in the field often means good
service.

4. *If the IRS calls me in for an audit, what should I do?*
Many people never actually talk with the IRS themselves. They let their CPA handle all contact with the
government.

5. *What personal records do I need to keep, and where
should I keep them?* Experts disagree on the best place
to store life insurance policies and wills, for instance.
Some suggest a safe deposit box; other suggest leaving them with a trusted professional advisor or in a
home strong box.

6. *Am I using the best filing status?* Some married people
file separately; most file jointly. The latter generally
will save you more in taxes, but not in all cases.

WHAT FEES YOU'LL PAY

Depending upon the complexity of your tax situation, the
type of service required, and the prevailing rates in the area,
CPAs usually base their fees on the time needed to do the job.
Occasionally, an accountant will bill a flat fee for a tax return
with a certain number of schedules. (Each additional schedule
will cost more.) But, in general, CPAs bill by the hour. Staff
accountants who work under the supervision of a CPA charge
anywhere from $50 to $175 per hour; higher level employees
such as a supervisor, manager, or partner charge $225 per hour
and up.

In addition, you'll be billed for the CPA's out-of-pocket expenses, such as long-distance phone calls, faxes, and photocopies, that arise from handling your particular tax problem. Ask the CPA in advance what expenses he'll charge you for, and at what rate.

To avoid any misunderstanding involving the fees charged, ask the CPA for an *engagement letter*. This spells out in advance what services the CPA will do, and what he'll charge. If the CPA quotes you an hourly fee, get him to estimate in this letter how long he expects the project to take him. If the CPA quotes you a flat fee, find out what's included for that one price. Attendance at an audit, for instance, is generally *not* included in the tax preparation fee.

In this lesson, you learned what a certified public accountant can do for you. In the next lesson, you will learn what a lawyer can do for you.

WORKING WITH A LAWYER— PART 1

In this lesson, you will learn what a lawyer can do for you.

WHAT LAWYERS ARE SUPPOSED DO

Lawyers have gotten a bad reputation lately. Perhaps it's because ours has become such a highly litigious society, with people suing each other upon the slightest provocation. Perhaps it's because lawyers charge outrageously high fees for even a five-minute phone conversation. And they talk and write in *legalese*, a language only they understand but in which all the laws and regulations are written. Perhaps it's simply because there are so many lawyers.

Whatever your real or perceived prejudices, lawyers provide a necessary service. They represent you, the consumer, in nearly every aspect of your daily life—everything from buying a house to paying debts to getting married—and put your best interests first. A lawyer's job, after all, is to protect your rights in any given legal situation.

Obviously, you don't need to talk to a lawyer about every little legal problem that arises. Some matters are best handled by simply talking them out with the other party or filing the legal papers yourself. Other problems may be solved in small claims court.

When should you contact a lawyer, then? Generally, when you're going through a major life change like a divorce or a death, or a shift in your financial status such as a pending bankruptcy or your home's foreclosure. According to the American Bar Association, in fact, the three most common legal problems taken to lawyers involve real estate, estate planning, and marital problems.

WHAT IS A LAWYER—AND WHAT CAN HE OR SHE DO FOR YOU?

A lawyer is a licensed professional who can advise and represent you in legal matters. He has two main duties: to protect your rights (as a client), and to uphold the law.

Like most people, when you think of the word *lawyer* you probably picture Perry Mason. Nothing could be further from the truth, however. Lawyers spend the lion's share of their working hours in the office—researching, writing, and preparing legal documents, giving advice, and settling disputes—rather than giving dramatic speeches in court.

Although many lawyers still operate as *general practitioners*, ready to handle just about any type of legal case, most lawyers specialize nowadays in one or two areas such as domestic relations, taxation, or real estate. Most general practitioners deal in civil practice (rather than criminal law). And half of the cases that they handle involve separation and/or divorce proceedings.

> **tip**
>
> **Beyond His Ability**   Much like a family doctor referring a cancer patient to an oncologist, a good lawyer will tell you if a particular case is beyond his expertise and refer you to a lawyer who specializes in that type of law.

What aspects of your financial life can a lawyer help you sort through? The following sections describe the most common situations.

Marriage and Divorce

A lawyer will draw up separation agreements and negotiate divorce settlements. (The latter is especially important if you and your spouse are fighting about the division of your assets.) He'll advise you on visitation and other rights of a child custody arrangement. He'll negotiate annulment, adoption, and foster care proceedings. He'll even help you figure out when you should consider a prenuptial agreement—and what property can and should be included.

Writing a Will and Estate Planning

A lawyer can draw up a will, a necessary document even for people with small "estates." Should you die "in testate" (without a will), your assets will be divided by the state rather than according to your wishes. To whom do you want to bequeath that diamond pendant—or the secret of your five-alarm chili? An often-overlooked clause in a will is a custody provision, which details who you want to raise your children should you and your spouse die.

A lawyer can also counsel you on "estate planning." Do certain family members need extra protection, like infants or the disabled? Will your immediate family be provided for? The number one reason, however, that clients call in a lawyer for estate planning is because he can help reduce their estate taxes significantly.

BUYING A HOME

A lawyer can represent you when buying or selling a home. If you're selling a home, your lawyer will *prepare* the contract of sale. If you're selling a home, your lawyer will *review* the contract of sale and negotiate the terms with the seller's attorney. (Seek his advice early enough in the process and a lawyer will help you negotiate the sale price, too.) In addition, a lawyer will review your mortgage loan commitment from the bank, make sure there are no liens against the property, and ensure that you get everything promised in the contract at the closing.

TAXES

A lawyer can advise you about your legal rights and obligations concerning local, state, and federal income taxes; local real estate and personal property taxes; and inheritance and estate taxes. He can also advise you on the tax consequences of capital gains on real estate; sales of appreciated stocks; bequests to spouses and children; charitable contributions; and pensions, trusts, and annuities.

In addition, he can advise you during a tax audit and represent you in tax court, if necessary.

PERSONAL FINANCES

A lawyer can get you back into the black. He'll help you re-structure your debt by arranging for a debt-consolidation loan or contacting your creditors and getting an extension on your loan payments. Sometimes he can even work out a deal with your creditors to settle your accounts with them for less.

He'll also help you clean up your credit file. If your house is in foreclosure, he'll push for a "forbearance agreement," which extends your payments and prevents you from losing the house. Creditors hounding you every waking moment? He'll counsel you on a bankruptcy filing.

> **!** **The Bottom Line**   A lawyer must find out what a client wants—to award their spouse as little as possible in a divorce settlement, for instance, or draft an ironclad prenuptial agreement—and then find ways *within the law* to do that.

THE NECESSARY CREDENTIALS

Lawyers must be schooled in how laws and the legal system work. Since so much of general law is based on state law, each state sets its own educational and professional standards. In most states, however, lawyers must meet the following require-ments before they can practice law:

- Earn a bachelor's degree from an accredited college.

- Earn a juris doctorate degree from an accredited law school.

- Pass a state bar exam. These rigorous, comprehensive exams require knowledge in all areas of the law, and in professional ethics and responsibility.

- Pass a character review. A committee checks out a candidate's background, looking for black marks such as past criminal activity and disbarment in another state.

- Get licensed. Each state supreme court issues licenses to would-be lawyers after they've met the above qualifications and have taken an oath to uphold the laws and the constitution.

A lawyer can practice law once he's licensed by the state in which he wants to work. However, being licensed in one state doesn't mean he can automatically practice law in a neighboring state, too. To do so, he must "petition for admission," but only after he's practiced law in the state in which he's licensed for at least five years.

Lawyers have been slow to specialize—officially, that is. Most lawyers are better schooled in one area of the law than another, but they may not advertise that fact. (In some states, they're prohibited from doing so.) Some states now "certify" attorneys who specialize in areas like bankruptcy, domestic relations, tax, estate planning, and real estate through programs that they've set up. To qualify, a lawyer must have attended continuing education classes, practiced in his field of expertise for at least 10 years, and passed an additional exam. Some private organizations, such as the American Bankruptcy Board and the National Association of Estate Planning and Counsel, will also certify lawyers in their speciality.

> **tip** **Not Just a Name**   Anyone who calls himself a
> *lawyer*—or an *attorney, barrister, counsel, counse-*
> *lor*, or *solicitor*—is licensed. Legally, they can't use
> the name otherwise.

In this lesson, you learned what a lawyer can do for you. In
the next lesson, you will learn how to find a lawyer, and also
about the fees that lawyers charge.

WORKING WITH A LAWYER— PART 2

In this lesson, you will learn how to find a lawyer, and also about the fees that lawyers charge.

HOW TO FIND A LAWYER

Ask friends, relatives, and business acquaintances for references. However, remember that the lawyer who handled your best friend's divorce may not necessarily be the best person to draw up your will. Sometimes the lawyer you've been referred to may actually refer *you* to another lawyer in the firm who specializes in your particular problem.

If that doesn't work, call a referral service. The service will usually recommend a lawyer in your area who specializes in your problem. But many services will refer you to *all* the lawyers who are members in a particular organization, meaning you'll be given names of lawyers with varying degrees of experience and specializations. To find a referral service, look in the telephone book under "Lawyer Referral Service." Check your local or state bar association, too. The association usually runs a lawyer referral and information service.

> **tip**
>
> **Hotline Help**   The American Association of Retired Persons (AARP) offers a free legal hotline service. A practicing attorney will answer basic legal questions and, if necessary, refer you to a lawyer in your area. Call AARP at 800-424-3410 for the hotline number in your area. Not all states offer the service, however. Those areas that do: Florida, Arizona, Texas, California, Hawaii, Kansas, Ohio, Pennsylvania, Maine, Michigan, Missouri, Washington, D.C., and Puerto Rico.

Lawyers are now permitted to hawk their services in TV, radio, and newspaper advertisements, even the telephone book. Can you believe everything you hear? No more—or less—than you can believe an advertisement for soap or gasoline. Many ads will trumpet the lawyer's specialty (which is helpful). Others may even quote a fee or price range. Generally, however, these prices are for the "simplest" cases—and they rarely exist.

> **!**
>
> **No Fee Unless...**   ...unless we win your case. By making such a claim, the lawyer isn't pulling a fast one, exactly. The truth is, if he doesn't think he'll win the case, he probably won't take you on as a client.

Even the best referral can't guarantee a lawyer's integrity, however. Contact the State Bar to see if the lawyer is in good standing. Generally, unethical lawyers are disbarred for a period of time. (Some are disbarred forever, however.) The most common reason for disbarment: misusing the client's funds.

If, after you hire someone, you're not satisfied with the legal counsel provided or you think your lawyer has acted unethically, you can take the following steps:

- *Fire your lawyer.* You may be charged a reasonable amount for the work already done. But most of the documents involved in the case belong to you. Ask for them.

- *File a complaint.* Contact the city, county, or state bar association. Many of these associations now have an office set up to investigate consumer complaints. If you believe that you were charged extraordinary fees, the state or city bar association's fee arbitration service will handle your complaint.

- *Get your money back.* Contact the state "client security fund" if you feel that a lawyer has improperly kept your money. This fund, also called a "client indemnity fund" or a "client assistant fund," is set up to compensate consumers who are defrauded by lawyers.

- *Sue for malpractice.* If the lawyer's been negligent in handling your case—and it cost you money—you may have a case against him.

SEVEN *REALLY* GOOD QUESTIONS TO ASK A LAWYER

Before you retain a lawyer's services, ask him or her the following questions:

1. *How long have you been practicing law?* Does he specialize in any particular area of the law?

2. *What kinds of legal problems do you handle most frequently?* How many divorce cases (or tax or real estate or whatever your concern is) has he handled in the last year, for example? What's his success rate?

3. *What's your schedule like?* What you're trying to find out is if he's too busy to give your case the attention it needs.

4. *Who will be working on my case?* Paralegals and other non-lawyer assistants often do much of the research and preparation. If these assistants are used, will you be charged separately for their services? Generally, paralegals bill at a lower rate than an attorney. Ultimately, the attorney may charge more for his services, though, because he has a large staff on his payroll.

5. *What is the most likely outcome of this case?* Naturally, a lawyer can't guarantee a big settlement, nor does he work with a crystal ball, but he can give you his opinion about the case's strengths and weaknesses.

6. *How much will this cost, and how long will the work take?* Find out what method of payment he uses and whether he expects payment up front or upon completion of the case.

7. *How will we communicate?* Find out how often he'll call you to keep you apprised of the case's progress. Will he send you copies of pertinent documents? What other information will he give you?

Legal Fees and Expenses

Legal advice isn't cheap. To draw up a simple one-page document or to offer general advice over the phone, a lawyer may charge you several hundred dollars. Ultimately, what you're paying for is the lawyer's expertise—the more specialized he is and the more years of practice he has under his belt, the more you'll probably pay—as well as the actual time spent working on your case. Still, to avoid any misunderstanding, get an estimate for his fee in writing if possible, and make sure you're clear about the method used to arrive at his fees.

 Retainer A retainer fee is a set amount of money paid regularly to a lawyer. In return, the lawyer offers routine consultation and legal advice, as needed.

Generally, retainers are used by corporations or businesses because they have a steady flow of legal issues that must be managed continuously. Like the average person, however, you probably need to hire a lawyer *periodically*. This year you need a lawyer to draw up a contract of sale on your house, for instance; next year you want a will; the following year you may need to set up a trust; and so on.

Frequently, a lawyer will ask for some money up front. Although he may refer to this as a "retainer," it's really just a down payment. You'll receive regular statements, which break down his charges, and which tell you when his fees have exceeded the initial retainer. At that point, you can either stop working with him, or continue the case.

An *hourly-rate fee* means that a lawyer charges a set amount—ranging from $150 to $300, but it could be even higher if a lawyer is a well-known expert in some aspect of the law—for every hour that he spends working on your case. For individuals, it's the most common way to be billed for legal services.

When does the clock start ticking?

Immediately. Expect to be billed for every phone conversation, every letter written, and every minute spent researching your case or filing papers in court. Some lawyers may charge more for courtroom time than for hours spent researching. In general, though, larger law firms will charge more *per hour* than smaller firms; big-city lawyers will charge more than rural ones; and more experienced lawyers will charge more than inexperienced ones.

> *tip*   **Not Less Costly**   Inexperienced lawyers may charge less per hour than their more seasoned counterparts, but it may take them longer to complete the same job. Lower hourly fees, therefore, many not necessarily translate into more money in your pocket.

A *fixed fee* is a flat fee that will be charged for routine legal work. Often, you'll see this type of fee schedule offered in advertisements: Divorce—$200. Most likely, it'll cost you more. That price doesn't include court costs or other expenses.

Contingency fees are paid to a lawyer "contingent" upon the outcome of the case. In other words, the lawyer agrees to be paid a percentage (often one-third) of the amount of money that the client wins in the case settlement. Used most often in negligence cases involving personal injury, this fee arrangement is *not* used for the legal services covered in this book (marriage and divorce, wills and estate planning, taxes, personal finance, and real estate).

Referral fees are sometimes paid when you're referred by one lawyer to another. In these instances, the original lawyer may receive a portion of the total fee paid to the succeeding lawyer. This fee is often prohibited, however, unless you, the client, know about the arrangement and both lawyers actually do some work on the case. If you're referred from one lawyer to another, ask whether a referral fee will be paid.

MISCELLANEOUS EXPENSES

Some costs and expenses will be charged in addition to your fee. *Costs* generally refer to postage, long-distance telephone calls, xerox copying of documents, and other expenses not included in the legal fee. Expenses may include the fee paid to the sheriff's office for serving a summons, or the fee charged for filing a complaint with the court clerk's office.

Generally, you'll be billed for these items as they occur. Sometimes, a lawyer will run a tab, billing you for the total amount after his work is completed.

In this lesson, you learned how to find a lawyer and how a lawyer is paid. In the next lesson, you will learn about low-cost alternatives to legal services.

WORKING WITH A LAWYER— PART 3

In this lesson, you will learn about alternatives to traditional legal counsel and what to do when you can't afford an attorney.

WHEN YOU SHOULD HIRE AN ATTORNEY

Contacting a lawyer every time you have a "legal" issue can be time-consuming, expensive, and downright unnecessary. Some consumers will literally make every issue a *federal* case, dragging their problems to the highest court possible. Others try to take on too much themselves, and *then* call a lawyer to bail them out, after they've signed most of their rights away.

Obviously, some matters are simply so complex that you absolutely *must* hire a lawyer to handle them. But a good many cases—especially uncontested divorces, basic boilerplate wills, and simple real estate deals—can be resolved without a lawyer's help or, at the very least, settled out of court.

Alternatives to Traditional Legal Counsel

Unless your legal problem is clearly of a very complicated or serious nature—and only a lawyer will do—you might consider using one of the alternative methods described in the following sections rather than seek traditional legal counsel.

Dispute Resolution Centers

Dispute resolution centers help consumers resolve common problems outside the courtroom. They're also known as *neighborhood justice centers, citizens' dispute settlement programs,* and *night prosecutor's programs.*

Each center differs in procedure and effectiveness. The goal is to encourage people to discuss their problems openly with each other—and with the help of a neutral mediator. A more formal process called *arbitration* settles disagreements quickly and inexpensively. (Some centers offer the service gratis.)

> **!** **Decision Is Final** Both sides must present their evidence and witnesses (if any) to a presiding arbitrator, who will ultimately grant a decision. The trouble is, both parties involved must agree in advance to accept the arbitrator's final decision. Unlike a real court case, appeals are not permitted.

SMALL CLAIMS COURT

Small claims court, on the other hand, is a special, simplified court that lets you handle your own case without a lawyer. Often, this is a good choice if you're being sued, or are suing another party, for a small amount. Small claims court is also known as *magistrate courts, justice of the peace courts,* and *pro se courts.*

Each small claims court differs from state to state. There's a limit on how much money you can seek, ranging from $200 to several thousand dollars. Although a judge presides over the case, there is no jury. You act as your own attorney, so the cost is low. The simplified process keeps complicated forms and other paperwork to a minimum. And the cases are processed quickly; often a case is filed, argued, and decided within three months.

> *tip*   **Time Limits**   Every state has a time limit—technically it's called the "statute of limitations"—within which a case must be filed. Time limits vary for different types of cases. To find out exactly how much time you have to file a particular lawsuit, ask the small claims court.

PRO SE REPRESENTATION

Pro se—or self-help—means that you represent your own case. This method is used most commonly in simple divorce proceedings and other cases involving family law.

A do-it-yourself divorce involves filing the necessary papers at the clerk's office at the courthouse—that's where you can pick up the papers initially, too—and appearing before the judge at a hearing to explain why you want a divorce. In Arizona, Utah, and most recently California, where the process is more state-of-the-art, it's even easier. For about $30, computerized divorce kiosks guide divorcing couples through 90 or more pages of legal documents tailored to their county's law. Once completed, the couple can head over to the courthouse, print-out in hand.

! **Not Advisable**   Cases in which the husband and wife are battling over the division of property, or the joint estate is an especially complicated one, require a lawyer's expertise. A husband and wife can both use the same family attorney to represent them unless there's a conflict of interest. Another reason to opt for legal counsel? Judges generally dislike *pro se* cases because it means they must deal directly with consumers who are unschooled in the workings of the law. A judge might look more kindly upon you ultimately if your side of the case is represented by counsel.

Basic boilerplate wills are another good choice for do-it-yourself counselors. Bookstores abound with self-help tomes addressing this subject, and many office supply stores now carry "Last Will and Testament" forms.

tip **Cyber Savvy**   If you're computer literate, try one of these easy-to-use software packages. Quicken American Lawyer (800-223-6925) prepares 74 legal documents such as a power of attorney, a premarital agreement, and a residential real estate lease. The program features an "Interview," which creates documents based on answers to questions much like an attorney would ask. If you need help with estate planning, try Willmaker and Living Trust Maker, both from Nolo (800-992-NOLO).

But wills are cheap—often as low as $100—even when they're drafted by an attorney. Why? Most lawyers view wills as a "loss leader." It's a good first step to winning you as a client. Having drawn up your will, the lawyer will hopefully see it through probate (which is when he earns heftier fees) and, should you need an attorney for some other matter in the future, he's hoping you'll call on him again.

REAL ESTATE BROKERS

You may not need a lawyer when buying or selling your house, either. There is a growing trend, in fact, to allow real estate brokers in every state to act as escrow agents in a lawyer's place. (Some states already permit this practice.) Obviously, the absence of a lawyer's fee will lower your closing costs.

But a real estate broker—no matter what he says—doesn't represent *you*. Only a lawyer does. Since a home is often the biggest investment that most consumers make, you might do better in the long run—especially if it's a somewhat complex deal—by hiring an attorney to read over the contract of sale for you.

Three Smart Ways to Save Money on Legal Fees

Good legal advice is generally quite costly. But you can help keep your legal costs down by following some of these money-saving tips:

1. *Do some of the work yourself.* Called "unbundling," this practice keeps legal fees down by letting you do some of the legwork, such as gathering documents and other research, compiling the names and addresses of witnesses, and making phone calls.

2. *Keep it short.* Your lawyer is running a tab, billing you for every single phone call and meeting, regardless of what you actually talk about. Don't chat about the weather—or how badly the local team is doing this season—unless you're willing to pay $200 per hour for it.

3. *Be honest.* Give your lawyer all the facts about your case up front. It'll save time—and money—that would likely be spent later on investigation.

When You Can't Afford a Lawyer

If you're accused of committing a crime, the U.S. Constitution guarantees that you'll get a lawyer even if you can't afford to pay for legal counsel. There's no such law, unfortunately, for civil cases. Although attempts have been made over the last two decades to ensure that everyone—the poor especially—has access to legal counsel for *all* types of cases, free or reduced-cost services for divorce, bankruptcy filing, and estate planning are still hard to come by. The following options are not extended to every consumer, but they're certainly worth investigating if you're short on funds.

LEGAL CLINICS

Legal clinics process routine cases, generally relying on standard forms and paralegal assistance. The cost is relatively low. This is often a good choice if you want a will, a divorce, or a bankruptcy filing.

You'll find clinics listed in the yellow pages, but most often you'll hear about them on television. (They rely heavily on such advertising.) Local and state bar associations often run clinics periodically, which focus on a particular legal issue such as divorce or bankruptcy.

LEGAL AID PROGRAMS

Legal aid programs offer free legal counsel to the poor. To qualify, you must be living at the poverty level—or a fraction above—as defined by the U.S. Government. That means you didn't earn more than $9,000 last year ($18,000, if you're supporting a family of four).

To find a legal aid program in your area, look in the yellow pages under "Legal Services" or "Legal Aid." Or, call your local or state bar association for a referral. Some charitable organizations such as the Salvation Army also offer legal services in many communities around the country. You might even try calling a local attorney. Explain that you don't have any money and that you're looking for a legal aid program. He should be able to locate one for you.

Most legal aid offices have staff lawyers of their own as well as support from paralegals and other assistants. Some offices also use the services of private practice lawyers who volunteer their time.

PRO BONO PROGRAMS

Pro bono service is legal counsel given *for free* by private practice lawyers to low-income clients. How low is low-income? That depends. Unlike legal aid, *pro bono* programs don't set out specific income guidelines. They consider your income as well as the legal problem itself and your family situation. Women who are victims of domestic violence, for instance, are frequently offered *pro bono* services for divorce proceedings.

Approximately 1,000 organized *pro bono* programs are currently being administered by local legal services offices and the local and state bar associations. The Legal Aid Society in New York City, for instance, offers *pro bono* services for wills and estate planning to AIDS patients. The Legal Services Corporation of Iowa, for example, offers *pro bono* services for eviction, custody, and other civil cases. In addition, many law firms, especially the larger ones, run *pro bono* programs.

tip   **Student Help**   Many law schools offer no-cost programs, too, in which their students provide *pro bono* services.Pro Bono Students America, a clearinghouse of student *pro bono* work nationwide, is operated out of New York University School of Law.

Since it's not mandated by law, what compels some lawyers to offer their services for nothing? Ethically, lawyers are supposed to offer legal counsel to everyone—even if that *everyone* can't always pay. It's all part of that code of ethics they promise to uphold when they receive their license. Some lawyers take that code to heart: doing a *pro bono* case enables them to do some public service. Other lawyers could care less, or else are too distracted by the "for profit" side of their business.

REDUCED-COST SERVICE

Reduced-cost service is a more reasonably priced fee offered to middle-income clients who generally make too much money to qualify for *pro bono* or legal services yet are too cash-poor to afford the full cost of retaining a private-practice attorney. Most of the low-fee programs currently in existence are offered through the local and state bar associations.

In this lesson, you learned about alternatives to traditional legal counsel and what to do when you can't afford an attorney. In the next lesson, you will learn what a national tax-preparation chain can do for you and when you should consult an enrolled agent.

WORKING WITH A TAX SPECIALIST

In this lesson, you will learn what a national tax-preparation chain can do for you, and when you should consult an enrolled agent.

PREPARING A TAX RETURN

Anyone can prepare a tax return. Each form comes with step-by-step instructions. And, should you get stuck, the IRS even offers over-the-phone assistance. But add to that simple tax return a lengthy list of deductions, a home (or even more confusing, a rental property), and a tax language that sounds like Sanskrit, and you're hopelessly lost. Also, no matter how thorough you are, you always have this fear that you've somehow missed something.

Of course, you could pay someone else to do the job for you. But who? A tax *attorney*, or a tax *accountant*? An enrolled agent, or one of those national chains? And just how much will it cost? Fees run the gamut—anywhere from $50 to several hundred dollars, depending upon the complexity of your return and who you hire to prepare it. Tax attorneys and tax accountants, for example, tend to charge substantially more than an enrolled agent or a national tax-preparation chain.

Still confused? You're not alone. About half of the 116 million people who file a return each year go to a tax professional.

NATIONAL TAX-PREPARATION CHAINS

What can a national tax-preparation chain (such as H&R Block) do for you?

In March and April, national tax-preparation chains such as H&R Block are very busy. With nearly 10,000 offices in operation, H&R Block, for instance, processed 17.5 million personal tax returns last year. Their average charge: $70 per return. (Fees vary, however, depending on the amount of work done.)

These tax-preparation services usually file the returns electronically, which will speed up your return. In addition, some chains offer an "instant refund." This is actually a loan made against your anticipated federal income tax refund. The fees for such "refunds" can run pretty high: $29 for a $200 to $500 loan; $60 for a $501 to $1,500 loan; and $89 for a $1,501 to $3,500 loan.

National chains are convenient, too. They have offices set up all over the world, in most major cities, even small, rural areas such as Chinook, Montana, and Island Falls, Maine. And you don't even have to set up an appointment. Most often they dole their advice out on a first-come, first-serve basis until the last customer's return has been filed on April 15th.

The drawback? The agent you worked with last year may not work there this year, or else he's probably busy reviewing another client's return. The prices are so cheap because you're not getting the personal service that you do with a private accountant or financial planner. Plus, although an H&R Block agent will *accompany* you to an audit, he generally cannot go in your place.

ENROLLED AGENTS

Don't be misled by the name. An enrolled agent does *not* work for the Internal Revenue Service (or "The Service," as people in the field refer to it). Nor does he sell life insurance. Rather, an enrolled agent is a tax expert who specializes in representing consumers before the IRS. That's what he is licensed to do by the federal government, in fact.

To earn his E.A. credential, an enrolled agent must have either worked for the IRS at least five years in some tax-related capacity (he couldn't have just worked as a file clerk, for instance, to qualify), or else passed a rigorous two-day exam given by the IRS which focuses solely on taxation.

An enrolled agent is not a CPA. But he is an expert in all areas of tax preparation. Some even specialize in preparing returns for certain professions, like the self-employed, civil service workers, or small business owners. To maintain his credentials, the enrolled agent must earn 72 hours of continuing education every three years.

WHEN YOU SHOULD CONSULT AN ENROLLED AGENT

Only about 1% of the tax-paying population is ever audited, but that isn't the only reason consumers are called before the IRS. An enrolled agent can help if you must talk to the IRS on the federal or state level about:

- *Taxes you owe that you cannot afford to pay.* Let's say that you owe $100,000 in taxes. But you're a single mother supporting two small kids on $25,000 per year. Since it's unlikely that you'll be able to pay the

IRS back *in full* in the near future, an enrolled agent
can help you arrange an "offer in compromise." Basically, your agent will propose to the IRS that they
reduce your tax bill to an affordable amount—maybe
$40,000, in this case—that you could pay *now*.

* *Collection efforts.* If you owe money to the IRS—and
can come up with the cash within a reasonable
amount of time—an enrolled agent will arrange a
realistic payment schedule for you.

* *Unusual circumstances.* You file a joint return with
your spouse, for instance, but last year he filed incor-
rectly. Are you liable, too? Perhaps there's a dispute
over a divorce settlement. You and your ex-spouse
have each declared your two children as dependents
on separate tax returns. Is any additional tax now
owed? Who's responsible for paying it?

Like a CPA and most other professionals, an enrolled agent's
fees vary with the complexity of the project as well as the going rates of such services in the community. Most enrolled
agents charge either a flat fee for tax preparation, or charge by
the hour for more complicated assignments. Their price?
About $75 to $100 per hour. That fee is heftier than a typical
tax-preparation chain's charge, but less than a CPA's fee, and
far less than an attorney's fee.

To find an enrolled agent or to find out more about the profession itself, contact the National Association of Enrolled Agents
at 200 Orchard Ridge Drive, Suite 302, Gaithersburg, MD
20878. Contact their 24-hour referral hotline at 800-424-4339,
and they'll send you a list of three agents in your area.

> **Finally...Some Good News**   Whether you em-
> ploy a CPA, an enrolled agent, or H&R Block, tax-
> preparation fees are deductible.

GET HELP FROM THE INTERNAL REVENUE SERVICE

Believe it or not, the IRS can actually help you. They won't fill out the actual tax return for you, but they do offer over-the-phone assistance, free of charge. Just call 800-829-1040 and experts will answer questions about everything from "What's deductible as a medical expense?" to "Can you still declare an 18-year-old child who works part-time as a dependent?" The two most frequently asked questions: "Where do I send my return?" and "When is it due?"

In addition, the IRS discusses 140 different tax topics such as filing an extension, figuring out the taxes for household employees, and reporting unemployment compensation via its recorded TeleTax line (800-829-4477). They offer 100 free self-help tax booklets that can be ordered—along with the necessary tax forms—by calling 800-TAX-FORM. The computer literate can download all of this information by visiting the IRS's home page at **http:\\www.irs.ustreas.gov** on the World Wide Web. You can also dial the Internal Revenue Information Services (IRIS) Web site directly via modem at 703-321-8020.

Come tax season, the IRS frequently offers "walk-in assistance" to consumers who visit one of the IRS offices located across the country. (They're located in large cities mostly, such as Los

Angeles and New York.) Often, those same offices will also offer tax-preparation clinics. (This is not one-on-one assistance, however; if you have a complex return, you need a *paid* tax preparer.)

THE TAX ATTORNEY VS. THE CERTIFIED PUBLIC ACCOUNTANT

Let's assume that you have a *really* complicated tax situation. Your Uncle George just died, leaving you his cache of blue chip stocks, which have quadrupled in value since he bought them 20 years ago. You're obviously concerned about paying capital gains and inheritance taxes, but who should you call for help: an attorney or an accountant?

Both advisors can probably offer guidance in the above situation, but you may be better off with a CPA. Why? He charges less per hour. And he can prepare your tax return. Attorneys— even those that specialize in tax—*cannot* prepare tax returns.

So when should you hire a tax attorney? If you're involved in a serious tax dispute with the Internal Revenue Service that is being settled in tax court. Your CPA may have represented you, for example, before the IRS during an audit—even during the administrative appeal process. But once your appeal reaches tax court, you need a tax attorney to represent your interests. You should also hire an attorney if you have an extremely complex estate plan.

CHECKING UP ON A TAX PREPARER

Checking on a tax preparer isn't easy. The IRS publishes the names of CPAs, enrolled agents, and lawyers who are currently disbarred or suspended from practice before the IRS in its weekly Internal Revenue Bulletin (IRB). But unless you know the details of how and when your preparer got into trouble— and you also have a subscription to the IRB—finding the right bulletin is akin to finding that proverbial needle in the haystack. You can always check with your local Better Business Bureau, however, to see if any complaints have been filed against a particular tax advisor.

Of course, you could always take the direct approach. Ask your tax advisor if he's ever been suspended by the IRS or served some other disciplinary action. Otherwise, you might keep these "tips" in mind before hiring someone to prepare your taxes:

- *Beware solo practitioners.* If an accountant or an enrolled agent is on vacation, sick, or just "mysteriously" out of the office for a few weeks, you could find yourself in a jam if you need help *now*. Most reputable solo advisors arrange for other solo practitioners to answer their client calls when they're unavailable for extended periods of time.

- *Ask questions—in advance.* How much does he charge? Will he just fill out the necessary forms for you, or will he offer some advice, too? Will he repay you for any penalties that result from an error he makes? Will he accompany you to an audit? The time to find out the answers to these questions is *before* you hire him to prepare your taxes.

- *Avoid "magicians."* These guys don't care what receipts you actually have. If you're self-employed, they'll argue that deductions can be a certain percentage of your income—no matter what your records actually show. This won't stand up in an audit.

HANDLING AN AUDIT

Relatively few taxpayers are ever actually called for an audit by the IRS. But if you're one of the unlucky few to be summoned—your chances increase with your income level, by the way—you don't have to go alone. By law, taxpayers have the right to be represented at an audit by a CPA, a tax attorney, or an enrolled agent.

> **!** **No One Else Will Do**   You can bring the butcher, the baker, or the candlestick maker with you to an audit—if any of them happens to moonlight as a tax preparer—but they cannot go in your stead. Only attorneys, CPAs, and enrolled agents are licensed to appear in the taxpayer's place before the IRS.

Obviously, you'll have to pay for such representation. Most CPAs, for instance, will charge an additional fee to represent you at an audit should you be called. It's not included in their tax-preparation fee. BUT if the audit results from an error that the CPA himself made, often he'll pay the penalties levied, and sometimes the interest charged, too. A CPA (or any other tax preparer, for that matter) will never, however, pay the taxes owed.

Many audits are conducted by "correspondence" these days. In about one-third of these cases, the IRS merely sends you a letter with questions about a particular deduction or a calculation on your return. You (or your tax preparer) reply in writing, with the proper explanations and documentation. Unless there's some problem, that's it. The matter is settled.

"Field" and "office" audits are not quite so simple. (In a field visit, the IRS visits you, the taxpayer, at your place of business; in an office visit, you must visit an IRS office.) If you're called in for an office visit—and you had a CPA, an enrolled agent, or a tax attorney prepare your return—try to send that person in your place. Many tax preparers prefer to face the IRS *without* you, in fact, because they're afraid that you'll blurt something out that will hurt your case.

> **!** **Know Your Rights**   Taxpayers do have certain rights during an audit process. If the questioning gets tough and you're unsure how to answer, you can adjourn an audit meeting at any time, for instance, to consult a tax advisor. Similarly, if you're questioned about issues that are not related to your original notice, you can ask for extra time to gather the appropriate documentation. (For a complete list of your rights, check IRS Publication 1.)

In this lesson you learned what a national tax-preparation chain can do for you, and when you should consult an enrolled agent. In the next lesson, you will learn what to expect from a mortgage broker.

WORKING WITH A MORTGAGE BROKER

In this lesson, you will learn what to expect from a mortgage broker.

THERE REALLY ARE MORTGAGE BROKERS

Stockbrokers buy and sell *stocks*. Mortgage brokers buy and sell *mortgages*. Imagine that you want to buy a home. You've just found the house of your dreams, and the owner has accepted your offer. Now, you have to find a mortgage loan with which to pay for this house. But which lender will you go to? The savings bank down the street, or the big commercial lender in the city? Which type of loan will you pick? A 30-year fixed, or a 15-year adjustable?

You can do all of this comparison-shopping yourself. Call up a number of banks and get the interest rates and the points and the terms. Then fill out an application and attach the necessary documentation. Bring it to the lender. And wait for the results.

Or you can simply call up a mortgage broker and let him *find* you a loan. He'll do the comparison-shopping and loan processing. All you have to do is wait for the results.

What To Expect from a Mortgage Broker

Basically, a mortgage broker's job is to find loans for prospective homeowners like you. He knows almost everything there is to know about mortgages, so he can explain the various kinds of loans currently being offered. He can even help you pick the loan that best matches your needs.

Since a mortgage broker works with a variety of lenders on a regular basis, he's often an expert shopper. He'll find the best interest rates and the best loan products, sometimes uncovering deals that you would never hear about otherwise. If you have a complicated case—you've been job-hopping the past three years, for instance, or you're just starting out in your career and you don't earn that much money yet—a broker may be the *only* way you'll secure an affordable loan.

Once he finds the right loan for you, a mortgage broker will then "process" your loan. That means he'll do most of the upfront paperwork for you. He'll help you fill out the application and gather all the necessary and required documentation; verify your credit report and the home's appraisal; and submit the loan package to the lender. He'll even hold your hand while you sit anxiously awaiting the bank's approval of your loan.

THE MORTGAGE BROKER'S FEE

Naturally, a mortgage broker doesn't provide this service free of charge. But he doesn't charge you directly either, as most other financial advisors do. With mortgage brokers, you never have to pay an actual broker's fee. Instead, he'll attach his fee to the loan that you get.

Here's how it works: A mortgage broker buys loans at a wholesale price from banks and other institutions that lend money. Let's say that he buys a loan at 8%. When you stroll into his office the next morning looking for a mortgage, he may sell you that very loan he just bought. The only difference: he'll charge $8^{1}/_{2}$%. That's how a reputable broker makes his money—by buying low and selling higher.

Ideally, brokers should only beef up the points and interest rate on a loan so that it's comparable to other mortgage loans being offered directly by banks to consumers. (Otherwise, it's cheaper to buy directly from the bank.) Frequently, though, the broker's loan *beats* the bank loans that you can get directly. That means you may pay less for a loan bought through a mortgage broker than through a bank directly.

This probably sounds simple. If the bank is offering $8^{1}/_{2}$% on a mortgage and the broker is offering 9% on his mortgage, go with the bank. If the bank is offering 9% and the broker $8^{1}/_{2}$%, go with the broker. There's just one little problem, though. How will you know how much the bank is charging? You're not doing any of the research, remember. That's why you picked a mortgage broker in the first place, so that *he* would do all that work for you.

The truth is, even if you hire a mortgage broker, you're going to have to canvass some banks and other lending institutions to compare interest rates, points, and other costs of getting a loan. Otherwise, you won't know if you're getting the deal of a lifetime—or if you've just been hoodwinked.

Using newspapers, television, and the Internet and other online services, you can find out about mortgages and the current interest rates. It's easy to compare prices, in fact, if you're a model borrower. That is, you don't want anything fancy; you can put 20% down; and your credit rating is in good shape.

When comparing mortgages, your best bet is to look at the annual percentage rate of each loan. That way you're comparing like terms.

Annual Percentage Rate (APR)   The annual percentage rate is the cost of a mortgage as an annual rate. The APR is usually higher than the advertised interest rate because it includes interest, points, and other finance charges.

tip   **Quick Roundup**   To find the best mortgage deals in your area, order HSH Associates' Homebuyer's Mortgage Kit (800-873-2837; $20), which reports on up to 80 lenders, depending upon the area covered. You'll receive data about the interest rate, points, application fees, and other fees charged by each lender. Best of all, this mortgage information is updated weekly.

FINDING A MORTGAGE BROKER

When you're choosing a mortgage broker, it's important that you get a personal reference. Try the usual channels: get referrals from your family and friends, coworkers, and other professionals that you know, such as your lawyer or accountant. You can also contact the National Association of Mortgage Brokers. They'll give you a list of brokers in your area. (Write to them at: 1735 N. Lynn Street, Suite 950, Arlington, VA 22209.) No matter how you've selected other financial advisors in the past, this is *not* the time to pick a name randomly out of the phone book.

In general, mortgage brokers have bad reputations. In the past, mortgage brokers were generally the last resort of homeowners whose credit was so shaky they couldn't get a mortgage on their own. Brokers charged borrowers interest rates that were substantially higher than the going rate. But as one savings and loan institution after another failed, mortgage brokers started taking their place as low-cost originators of loans. Today, mortgage brokers arrange over half the mortgage loans issued nationwide every year. Generally, the loans they offer are competitive—if not cheaper—than the loans made by banks.

So why hasn't the public's perception of mortgage brokers kept up with the times? Because it takes time to change the image of an entire profession—and there are obviously still some unscrupulous operators out there. What should you do, then, to protect yourself?

Get a referral. If you can't, ask the broker himself for some former clients you may speak to. (One creative mortgage broker places a binder, filled with referral letters, in his office's waiting area for prospective customers to leaf through.) Try to find someone who's been in the business for at least five years. And be sure to do your homework.

An unscrupulous broker might try to hit you with lots of extra fees. One way to avoid that is to carefully read the "Good Faith Estimate" of costs associated with your loan, such as the number of points, the application fee, the credit check, appraisal fee, and private mortgage insurance. (By law, all brokers must now disclose this information to you within three business days of filing your application.) Later on, the broker can't charge you for a warehouse fee, for instance, if it's not listed on the Good Faith Estimate.

Most states require that mortgage brokers be licensed. But that may not mean much. In some states, brokers simply have to pay a fee to get licensed; in others, they must pass a test and meet other requirements. You can check by calling your state's Banking Department.

tip

Cyber Savvy   If you're an Internet user, you may want to tap into the "Mortgage Rate Shopper," offered by the United Homeowners Association (UHA). On the UHA's Web site, you can post some basic information about the type of mortgage you're looking for. Mortgage brokers, who monitor the page, will respond if they have the loan you want. You're not computer literate? The UHA will post the information for you. Just call 800-816-2870 for the correct form.

In this lesson, you learned what to expect from a mortgage broker. In the next lesson, you will learn how insurance is sold and how to select an insurance agent.

WORKING WITH AN INSURANCE AGENT—PART 1

In this lesson, you will learn how insurance is sold and how to select an insurance agent.

PAYING FOR PEACE OF MIND

Paying hundreds, maybe even thousands, of dollars to buy insurance every year sure seems like a waste of money. Until your house goes up in flames, the car is totaled in an accident, or some other disaster strikes. Then it seems like the smartest investment you ever made. When you purchase an insurance policy, what you're really buying is some peace of mind that you, your family, and your belongings are protected. And the more you have to protect, the more you'll spend on insurance.

That much you probably know already. The trouble is, you may have no idea how much coverage you actually need, nor whom to ask about it. You may automatically get health and life insurance on the job, so you haven't had much experience talking with insurance agents. Maybe you don't even know how to start shopping for insurance—never mind comparison shopping—since it's not immediately obvious where you buy insurance products, and how to go about doing so.

THREE KINDS OF INSURANCE

There are many different types of insurance and an even greater number of companies that sell it. But, in general, most consumers need at least three types of insurance:

- *Life Insurance.* Most people buy life insurance to replace the income that would be lost when you, or another family wage-earner, dies. You need life insurance most when you have dependents—e.g., young children or an aged parent.

- *Car Insurance.* You're required by law to have a minimum amount of car insurance (it varies by state). Basically, you want to be covered in case of an accident—no matter who's at fault—because the liability costs incurred in an accident can be exorbitant.

- *Homeowners Insurance.* You must have homeowners insurance to buy a house. The typical homeowners policy covers the house itself—as well as many of the belongings you keep in it—against fire and lightning, theft and vandalism, and several other "perils."

Property and Casualty Insurance   Property and casualty insurance is a term commonly used for car and homeowners insurance.

Two Kinds of Insurance Agents

Some 3,500 insurance companies currently sell homeowners and auto insurance in the United States. Another 1,800 or so companies sell life insurance. They all sell their products in two basic ways, however: either *directly* to the general public, or *indirectly* through independent insurance agents.

Companies that sell directly are called *direct writers*. You can buy an insurance policy directly from the company, or from a company agent. The person who sells you the policy might be salaried or work on commission, or both. But in all cases, you'll be dealing with a full-time employee of the insurance company.

Companies that sell indirectly are called *agency companies*. Unlike a direct writer, an agency company does *not* have its own sales force of insurance agents. Instead, these companies sell their policies through independent (that is, self-employed) agents. Typically, these agents work on commission and, since they represent several insurance companies, can give you rates and policy terms for a variety of insurers.

tip **Broker vs. Agent** You may have heard the term "broker" used in regard to insurance, too. But most likely you don't need his services, since insurance brokers generally deal with commercial rather than personal insurance.

Which is better—a direct writer or an agency company? That depends on whom you talk to. Since each of these agents is competing for your business, you're bound to hear from one that the other isn't looking out for the consumer's best interest and that the other charges heftier fees, and vice versa.

The truth is, both types of agent have their good (and bad) points. Direct agents are usually more familiar with company procedures (since they work for only one company), so they can probably process claims faster. Sometimes, these policies are cheaper, too, because these agents earn smaller commissions. Independent agents, on the other hand, can give you more objective advice about policies and prices since they don't work for any one company. These agents can even comparison-shop similar policies for you among several insurers.

So which is *really* better? Neither one. You may feel more comfortable with an independent agent, for example, than a direct writer, so by all means try to work with that type of agent. Ultimately, the most important feature to consider is *not* the type of agent, but the insurance policy itself. Does it meet your current needs? Is it affordable?

> ***tip*** **Insurance Hotline**   Contact the National Insurance Consumer Helpline (800-942-4242) for free advice about life, auto, and homeowners insurance. Sponsored by insurance industry trade associations, the hotline is staffed with insurance pros who'll tell you what to do if you're having trouble filing a claim, and how to buy insurance if you need it.

Finding an Agent

How do you find a reputable agent? An obvious first step is to ask around. What kind of insurance do your friends, relatives, and coworkers have? Who did they buy it from? Are they pleased with the service?

Another good source is the state insurance department or commission that regulates insurance companies and agents in your state. Many of these agencies publish consumer guides to insurance and cost-comparison surveys. Frequently, they'll also supply you with a list of agents in your area.

The following professional associations generally can offer some additional guidance, too:

- For auto and homeowners insurance, contact the state chapters of either the National Association of Professional Insurance Agents or the Independent Insurance Agents of America for the names and addresses of independent agents in your area.

- For life insurance, contact the American Society of CLU & ChFC at 888-CHFC-CLU; they'll randomly refer up to five chartered life underwriters in your area. Using its agent locator service, the local chapters of the National Association of Life Underwriters will likewise refer some of its member life insurance agents in your area.

You could always page through the yellow pages, of course. Both types of agent are listed in the yellow pages under "Insurance." In large cities such as New York, Chicago, and L.A., you'll find hundreds of names to pick from. But what if you've heard through the grapevine that such-and-such insurance company is good but they're not a direct writer? What you need is an independent agent who sells their products. Call the insurance company directly and ask the customer relations department how you can get in touch with an agent in your area who sells their product.

After getting some referrals, call or visit your top three prospects. Ask each agent what a particular policy would cost you and whether he offers any discounts. Auto insurers often offer discounts, for instance, to drivers who haven't had an accident in three years and to those who are over 50 years of age. Be sure to give exactly the same information about yourself to each agent. That way, you can realistically compare one agent's prices against prices from another agent.

In this lesson, you learned how insurance is sold and how to select an insurance agent. In the next lesson, you will learn what an insurance agent can do for you and what to expect when you file a claim.

WORKING WITH AN INSURANCE AGENT—PART 2

In this lesson, you will learn what an insurance agent can do for you and what to expect when you file a claim.

WHAT AN AGENT CAN DO FOR YOU

An agent should be ready, willing, and able to explain various insurance policies to you, and to answer all questions to your satisfaction. To determine your insurance needs, the agent will most likely ask you about your income and your background. (Do you have kids? Who else will be driving the car besides you? And so on.) Depending upon your answer—and the kind of insurance that you're buying—he can figure out how much coverage you and your family need and then recommend an affordable policy or two.

> **!** **Commission Confusion** When you purchase insurance, you generally pay a premium (or fee) every quarter. That's the price of the insurance; no other fees are involved. Whether or not your agent

works for a salary or a commission doesn't really matter. *You* never pay an agent a commission. The insurer does.

If you're buying life insurance, an agent will ask some additional questions about your health (your medical condition, for example, and your age and family medical history) and you may be asked to have a medical exam. Often, a licensed medical professional will visit your home.

When you buy life insurance, an agent can often provide a "policy illustration," which shows graphically how your policy will work. It's easier to understand how policy premiums, death benefits, cash values, and other variables work together when they're laid out in a chart.

tip   **Agents-Cum-Planners**   If you get general financial advice from your insurance agent, chances are that insurance—no matter what your problems are—will somehow figure into the solution. Whether it's buying a new policy or beefing up your existing coverage, insurance (in some form or another) is bound to be the mainstay of his advice.

Once you've bought a policy, you should touch base with your agent periodically to review your coverage. Obviously, you'd call him if you purchased a big-ticket item like a new home or car. But you should also notify him about somewhat smaller acquisitions, too, like that new computer and fax machine you put in your home office. (Does your homeowner's policy cover these items, for instance? For full value?) Remember to also notify your agent if a new baby has been born into the family, or your teenager just got her driver's license.

> **tip** **Purchase Protection**   When you purchase a policy, make your check payable to the insurance company, not to the agent. Be sure to get a receipt.

ELEVEN *REALLY* GOOD QUESTIONS TO ASK AN INSURANCE AGENT

Before you buy any type of insurance policy, make sure that you thoroughly understand the costs involved and the coverage that will be provided. When shopping for a policy, ask the insurance agent the following questions:

1. *What life insurance company(s) do you represent?*

2. *What kinds of insurance do you sell?* Although you're only in the market today for auto insurance, it pays to find out if the agent also sells homeowners insurance. You may want to add that coverage in the future.

> **tip** **Cheaper Rates**   Some companies that sell both auto and homeowners insurance will shave 5 to 15 percent off of your premiums if you buy two or more policies from them.

3. *How much are the premiums? And how frequently will they increase?* Some insurers raise their premiums

slightly every year; others ask for heftier increases after 18 months or more.

4. *What risk pool will I be assigned to?* High-risk candidates pay more. Many large insurance companies now offer *preferred* (lower) rates to low-risk customers.

5. *Does the insurer issue dividends to policyholders?* Some life insurance companies pay you dividends (cash) at the end of the year, depending on how well the company performed that year.

6. *What happens if I miss a payment?* Many insurers typically grant you a 30-day grace period.

7. *Can I add and/or make adjustments to this policy at any time?* In the near future, you may want to include an additional driver under your auto policy, or beef up your homeowners policy to cover your new home office equipment.

8. *When will the policy take effect?* Your first day of coverage may *not* necessarily be the date that the company issues the policy.

9. *Is my diamond tiara covered?* Generally, jewels valued over $1,000 require additional coverage. Ask about other atypical possessions, too, such as a stamp collection or a piece of artwork.

10. *How often will you review my policy to make sure that it's keeping up with my changing needs?* Ideally, he'll do this at least once per year.

11. *What am I responsible for, after I buy insurance?* Obviously, you must pay your premiums. But having auto insurance doesn't mean you can drive recklessly, or

that you don't have to bother filing a police report if you're involved in an accident. Similarly, if you remodel your house—add a second bathroom or install new windows, for instance—those changes should be documented on your homeowners policy.

Filing a Claim

You've been paying your insurance premiums, and all of a sudden, something happens. Who do you call? How do you file a claim?

If it's a theft or an accident, file a report with the police FIRST. If you don't, the insurer will probably deny your claim. Take photos of the damage—either to your car, your home, or yourself—if possible, and write down exactly what happened. Claims take time to process, and you're apt to forget many important details.

Then, notify your insurance agent and ask him what you should do next. He'll probably ask you to send him a copy of the police report and to fill out a one- or two-page claim form. In the meantime, he may also ask for many of the details over the phone so that he can get the claim process started.

If it's a homeowners claim (your roof was damaged by a wind storm, for instance), the insurer will send an adjuster to evaluate the damage within the week. If it's an auto claim (your car hit a tree), your insurer may ask you to get one or two repair estimates at local body shops. Larger insurers, however, usually send you to their own drive-in repair centers.

The result? Routine claims are often settled right away. More complicated cases can take up to three months.

Unfortunately, that's only half of the story. Insurers may reject your claim outright, saying that the damaged item isn't covered under your policy. Or they may agree to pay only a portion of the damage, again citing your coverage's restrictions as outlined in your insurance policy.

> ***tip***   **Check Your Policy**   Assuming that an insurer just automatically covers every emergency situation, or simply *should* pay for a tragic accident, is downright foolish. Read your policy carefully. It spells out the insurer's legal obligations to you, and under what circumstances.

When a claim is not settled to your satisfaction, you can just walk away (if the insurer is clearly acting within its rights). Or you can challenge the settlement, if you think that you have a case. Your first appeal should be to your agent. If that doesn't settle it, call the insurance company directly and ask for the claims department. Follow up your call with a letter, including any evidence such as a police report. Should the problem still not be resolved, your next step may be mediation, in which you and the insurer hire a "mediator" to settle the dispute for you.

You could always hire a lawyer who specializes in dealing with insurers, of course, to handle the matter for you. Sometimes all it takes, in fact, is one call from a lawyer to convince an insurance company to raise its settlement figure. (In the long run, the insurer figures it's cheaper than a court battle.) If not, your lawyer will likely take the matter to court. If you want to represent yourself (and save on legal fees), go to small claims court instead (see Lesson 7 for more details).

The Necessary Credentials

Most states require that agents be licensed to sell insurance, whether it's a homeowners policy or term life insurance. (To verify that your agent is licensed, contact your state Department of Insurance.) Agents who sell *variable* life insurance (policies that invest some of your premiums into money market funds, stocks, and/or bonds) must also be registered with the National Association of Securities Dealers in Washington, D.C. (800-289-9999).

Two professional designations to look for are Chartered Life Underwriter (CLU) and Life Underwriter Training Council (LUTC) Fellow. A CLU must pass ten college-level courses in individual life and health insurance, insurance law, and other related subjects at the American College in Bryn Mawr, Pennsylvania. CLUs must have at least three years of practical industry experience. Continuing education is also required.

An LUTC Fellow, however, is the top professional designation for a life insurance agent, conferred by the National Association of Life Underwriters. To qualify, an agent must be a member in good standing of a local association of life underwriters and have completed at least 300 credits in courses dealing with personal and business insurance.

Many life insurance agents belong to The National Association of Life Underwriters (NALU) in Washington, D.C. Through NALU's local associations, agents can attend educational seminars and stay abreast of new trends in the business. But no qualifying exam or educational background is required. Agents become members simply by paying a membership fee.

In this lesson, you learned what an agent can do for you and what to expect when you file a claim. In the next lesson, you will learn what a real estate agent can do for you, and when you should consider selling your house on your own.

WORKING WITH A REAL ESTATE AGENT

In this lesson, you will learn what a real estate agent can do for you, and when you should consider selling your house on your own.

REAL ESTATE TRANSACTIONS IN THE 1990s

It used to be so simple. Whether you were buying or selling your home, you called upon the local real estate agent to help you through the process. Not anymore. With the advent of sophisticated financing options, buying and selling a home has become more and more complex. And, now that housing prices are no longer enjoying the stellar returns they once did, consumers want to get their money's worth. Who does that agent really represent? Is my interest being protected?

All this has led to a great deal of confusion. Agents are playing lots of different roles nowadays, some of which are not very clear. Depending on whether you're the buyer or the seller, an agent can, on any given day, act as a buyer's agent, a seller's agent, a dual agent, even a subagent. For you, the consumer, this translates into different levels of loyalty and service—and additional savings if you negotiate these relationships properly.

Although 44 states now have "agency disclosure" laws that require real estate agents to disclose whom they represent, consumers are still confused. A recent survey commissioned by the National Association of Realtors found, in fact, that more than one-third of all buyers didn't know whom the agent represented after their first meeting. Here's the lowdown on what these various agents can do for you, and how to determine whom the agent represents.

THE SELLER'S AGENT

A seller's agent can guide you through every stage of the home-selling process—from setting a fair price to finding prospective buyers to reviewing the documents at the closing. He represents you, the seller, only.

> **!** **Don't Be Fooled** A seller's agent can help a buyer find a house. But although he may talk and act like he's your strongest ally, his loyalty is, ultimately, with the seller. That means he must try to get the highest price for the house, and he must pass along valuable negotiating information to the seller, such as whether the buyer really wants the house and, if pushed, whether he will pay more.

Before you even post that "For Sale" sign on the front lawn, an agent can help you get the most value for your home. Since he presumably knows the local housing market, a seller's agent can help you set the best price for your home. (Houses that are priced too high take longer to sell.) He may even advise you about simple ways to boost your home's appeal to potential buyers, such as putting a fresh doormat on the front porch, turning on a few extra lights, and simmering a pot of potpourri to create a homey atmosphere.

A seller's agent can expose you to a broader range of prospective buyers than you would probably find yourself. Agents generally list most homes with a multiple listing service, which lumps your home with numerous others in a network database that agents in a designated geographic area have access to.

What's more, a seller's agent is *objective*. A potential buyer is more apt to speak openly about what he likes about your house—and doesn't—with an agent rather than with you. A good agent will listen, perhaps suggesting changes that the seller might make if the house proves to be a difficult sell. A seller's agent can handle offers and counteroffers more objectively than you can, too.

The bottom line? An agent saves you the time and effort involved in selling your home. He lists the home, places the newspaper ads, fields telephone inquiries about the home, and arranges to show the home. (When the home is being shown, you can be teeing off at the golf course if you like. In fact, agents often prefer that the seller not be present.)

tip   **The Seller's Agent's Price of Service**   You must pay for this service, of course. Typically, 6% of the purchase price is paid as a commission by the seller to the agent.

THE BUYER'S AGENT

A buyer's agent is bound by contract to find a home and negotiate the lowest price and best terms for the buyer. As more
buyers learn that traditional agents don't represent their interests, they've begun looking for agents who do. Generally, a
buyer's agent will offer the same service that a seller's agent
does—saving you most of the legwork involved—only now the
client is *buying* real estate rather than selling it.

A buyer's agent can also help you determine how large of a
mortgage you'll qualify for, as well as what personal and financial data you'll need to bring when you apply for that mortgage. Some agents may be able to explain alternative financing
methods, too.

Buyer's agents are still fairly new, however. To avoid conflicts
of interest, some agents won't represent sellers—just buyers.
But most agents, especially sole practitioners, will represent
any client who walks through the door—either a buyer or a
seller.

tip   **The Buyer's Agent's Price of Service**   For an
exclusive buyer's broker, you'll pay about 3% of
the purchase price in commission. In most other
cases, you won't pay anything. The buyer's broker
will split the commission paid by the seller with the
seller's agent.

OTHER TYPES OF AGENTS

The subagent is the agent's *agent*. He brought in the successful
buyer—but he did not list the house originally.

Agents routinely work with other agents to find buyers for a seller's property. The agent that you work with directly is called the "listing agent" because he's the first to "list" the home. He may or may not bring in a buyer, however. Another agent across town might do that. He's then called the "sub-agent," or "selling agent," because he made the sale. In this case, that typical 6% commission is usually split between the listing agent and the subagent.

> **!** **No Subagent Allowed**   You can usually whittle that commission down by 1 or 2 percentage points, if you promise to give the listing agent an exclusive listing. The drawback: Since he's the only agent showing the house—rather than the many agents who normally would show it—it might take longer to find a buyer.

A facilitator is not an agent, exactly. He brings the buyer and the seller together, but he does not represent either party. A facilitator is fine—if you're comfortable doing most of the work involved with buying or selling a home yourself. Since you're getting less service, you should pay just 3% or less in commission.

Dual agents represent both the buyer and the seller in the same real estate transaction. Since the buyer seeks the lowest price and the seller the highest price, there is an apparent conflict of interest within this type of relationship.

While the law doesn't prohibit dual agency, the agent must clearly disclose to the seller that he's also working for the buyer, and vice versa. Often, dual agency occurs when the buyer's agent and the seller's agent work for the same real estate company.

> **tip** **The Dual Agent's Price of Service**   If you use a
> dual agent, you're getting less service, so by all
> means ask for a reduced commission: 5% instead
> of 6%, perhaps.

THE NECESSARY CREDENTIALS

A sales agent can help you buy or sell a home. In most cases, a sales agent works under the supervision of a real estate broker. All sales agents must be licensed by the state in which they work. Most states require agents to complete 30 hours of classroom instruction and pass an exam before awarding them a license.

A broker, on the other hand, is usually the person who owns the real estate firm. He can draw up the contract of sale for a home, in some states. In other states, only lawyers are permitted to do so.

Like agents, brokers must be licensed by the state, too. Most states require that brokers complete another 30 hours of classroom instruction and pass a separate broker's exam before receiving their broker's license. In addition, a broker must have logged at least one year's experience working as a sales agent.

Nearly 750,000 of the 1.2 million licensed real estate professionals out there belong to a local chapter of the National Association of Realtors, which is headquartered in Washington, D.C. To use the trademark REALTOR after their name, applicants must take a qualifying course and adhere to a strict code of ethics—in addition to earning a state license.

> **!** **Not Licensed** Some real estate professionals do operate without a license. It's illegal, but working with such an agent won't void your contract in most cases. You are not required to pay an unlicensed agent a commission, however, no matter what the contract says.

WHAT DO CONSUMERS THINK ABOUT REALTORS?*

- 78 percent of consumers believe real estate professionals can show buyers a broader selection of homes than they can find on their own.

- 74 percent agree that using a real estate broker saves time.

- 70 percent think that real estate professionals make buying or selling a home much easier.

Source: An independent survey of the general public released by the National Association of Realtors, Washington, D.C.

Figure 12.1   What do consumers think about realtors?

FINDING A REPUTABLE AGENT

Many people find an agent by accident. Either the person answers a newspaper ad for a home that the agent represents, or he spots a "For Sale" sign, listing the agent, posted on the front lawn of his dream house.

Some buyers-turned-sellers use the same agent that they worked with when they bought the house. Others get referrals from friends, family, neighbors, and coworkers.

You can also call your local real estate board. They'll refer you to Realtor members in your area. To find a buyer's broker, call the Buyer's Broker Registry in Ventura, California (805-492-8120), for a referral in your area.

SIX *REALLY* GOOD QUESTIONS TO ASK YOUR REAL ESTATE AGENT

Before you retain a real estate agent's services, ask him or her the following questions:

1. *Who do you represent—the buyer, the seller, or both?*

2. *What commission will you earn on this home sale?* Find out if he'll be sharing that commission with anyone else. If so, who? How much, if any, of that commission will you be expected to pay?

3. *What kind of services will you provide me if I want to sell my home?* Does he run ads, for instance? How frequently? In which publications? Does he use any online services? A multiple-listing service? Does he expect you to be at home when he shows the home?

4. *What kind of services will you provide me if I want to buy a home?* Will he have previewed all of the homes, for instance, before showing them to you to make sure that they fit your criteria? Will he be available to show you homes after work hours?

5. *How long have you been working as a broker or agent?* Also important: How many homes has he been the "selling agent" on over the last nine months? The "listing agent"?

6. *What can you tell me about the neighborhood?* Get a
   sense of what's available in and around town. Are
   there parks and other recreational facilities? How are
   the schools rated? What are the typical taxes like? Is
   it an incorporated village? Are there any community
   celebrations? And so on.

WHEN YOU DON'T NEED AN AGENT

You should think about selling your home on your own—
without the aid of an agent—if:

- *It's a seller's market.* This means that in your neighborhood, buyers outnumber the homes for sale.
  You're at an even greater advantage if your house
  falls in the mid-range of home prices in your neighborhood.

- *You're not in a hurry to sell.* You don't have to get the
  kids into their new school by September, or your
  spouse settled in a new job in another state. If you
  can wait till the right buyer comes along, you'll save
  several thousand dollars in commission.

- *You have plenty of time.* Time to run ads. Time to answer phone calls. Time to show the house.

In this lesson, you learned what a real estate agent can do for
you, and when you should consider selling your house on
your own. In the next lesson, you will learn what to expect
from a full-service stockbroker.

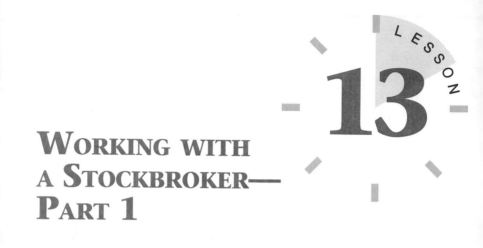

WORKING WITH A STOCKBROKER— PART 1

In this lesson, you will learn what to expect from a full-service stockbroker.

You're not an experienced investor. Up until now, you've probably socked away most of your extra cash into a certificate of deposit at the bank and your 401(k) plan at work. Lately, though, all you hear about is the *stock market*—and how much money people are making from it. Naturally, you'd like a little piece of the action, too. But does that mean you necessarily need a *stockbroker*? Can't you just invest in stocks and bonds yourself?

Not exactly. Should you decide to simply invest in a no-load stock mutual fund—yes, you can do that yourself. But to buy and sell individual stocks, bonds, and other securities on the "open" market, you need a broker to handle the transaction for you. How much that will cost you—and how much additional service you expect—will determine which kind of broker you choose. A full-service stockbroker, for example, will actually recommend stocks that you should buy. A discount broker won't—but you'll be charged far less in commission (the cost of trading a stock or other security). No matter which type of broker you choose, however, remember that they can't guarantee results. Risk is an unavoidable part of the stock market game.

What To Expect from a Full-Service Broker

All brokers buy and sell stocks for you. But a traditional broker, known as a *full-service broker*, will actually tell you which stocks to pick—and which to pan. He'll advise you about long-term investment strategies and risks, as well as manage your portfolio, provide periodic updates of your stock's performance, and send you reports from the brokerage's research analysts.

Basically, this guy is at your disposal whenever you need him. Your brother-in-law tells you at a New Year's Eve party that utility stocks are going to take a beating after the first of the year? Don't worry. If you have a full-service broker you can call him *immediately*, and ask him what to do.

Full-service brokers work for large, national firms such as Merrill Lynch, PaineWebber, and Prudential. These companies supply clients with every service and sell every financial product possible. Full-service brokers also work for smaller, *regional* firms like Edward Jones & Co. in St. Louis and Piper Jaffray & Hopwood in Minneapolis, which serve customers in a limited geographic area of the country.

The only problem with this "financial consultant" (that's how some full-service brokers bill themselves these days), however, is that there's often a serious conflict of interest at work. A stockbroker earns a commission on each "trade" that he places. (A trade is when he buys or sells a security for you.)

Typically, he keeps 30–40% of that commission himself; the rest goes to the brokerage firm. Obviously, the more trades that he makes, the more money the stockbroker earns.

That incentive system seems to work fine—until you remember that the stockbroker is supposed to put your investment interests *first*. Would this stock be a good addition to your portfolio? Should you hold these shares for the next three months? Ideally, a stockbroker should be buying (or selling) only those stocks that meet your financial objectives. In the real world, that doesn't happen as frequently as it should.

Here's why: Most brokerage firms demand a certain level of commission income—which usually requires a broker to buy and sell an awful lot of stock. Some firms dole out awards to brokers for overall sales production, or else circulate those production numbers throughout the office to keep up the pressure for high sales. Many firms even reward brokers who bring in hefty commissions with gifts or vacations. Ultimately, earning an impressive commission lands a stockbroker a vice presidency (or some other job promotion) at the firm.

It's no surprise, therefore, to discover that this constant pressure to earn a commission puts the broker's interest and the customer's interest (that's you) at odds. Underneath it all, your stockbroker is basically a salesman, and his earnings derive not from your investment success, but from how often, and how much, you buy and sell. Your broker may indeed take a personal interest in your finances and at times act like he's your best friend. But a stockbroker is focused primarily on one thing: To sell you stock or some other financial product that will earn him a commission. Chances are, therefore, that a broker may simply push products on you that aren't well-suited to your needs, but that earn him a hefty commission.

There's some other bad news, too. Remember that late-night call on New Year's Eve to check out those utility stocks? Unless you have a portfolio worth $100,000 or more, you probably won't rate such lavish attention. Your full-service broker will certainly call you back—but probably not till after the holiday.

WORKING WITH THE BROKER

To buy or sell stock with a full-service broker, you must first open an account. Usually, the broker will ask about your finances: savings, other investments, property owned, current debt load, investment goals. Why? To advise you, a stockbroker needs to understand your complete financial picture.

tip **Just Sign Here** Whenever you open a new account with a broker, you'll get a *disclosure statement*, which outlines all the risks you face investing in the stock market. Read it carefully before signing. And ask questions about anything that you don't understand.

If you plan on paying for the securities in cash, you can open a simple *cash account*. After buying a stock, you must pay your broker within three days (or you'll be subject to penalties up to $25). A *margin account* is for people who expect to borrow money from their stockbrokers so that they can buy more stocks than they could otherwise afford. (Borrowing on margin is risky, especially if you don't have the necessary funds to pay the stockbroker back when he puts a "margin call" on the account.) A *discretionary account* lets your broker buy and sell without getting your permission. (Eek! That's like telling a broker to rack up as many commissions as he wants.) A *joint account* lets both you and your husband tell the broker what to buy and sell.

After an account is opened, you can make a trade simply by phoning your broker. (You can visit a brokerage office in person, of course, if you prefer.) Once the order has gone through, you'll receive a *trade confirmation* in the mail, confirming what you bought, how much it cost, and the commissions you paid to the broker. When *you* pick a stock and ask your broker to buy it for you, that's called an *unsolicited order.* When *your broker* recommends the purchase of a particular stock, that's a *solicited order.*

In return for your stock or bond purchase, you receive an engraved certificate. (Treasury and some municipal bond purchases, however, are now registered by computer in a system known as *book entry.*) If you plan on doing a lot of buying and selling, you might want to store your securities with the brokerage firm. The shares will be registered in the firm's name, known as its *street name.* The firm's records, however, will clearly show that those shares belong to you.

COMMISSIONS AND OTHER FEES

Commissions are the bread and butter of this industry. The less often that you trade—and the lower your volume of trading—the higher your commissions per share will be. Conversely, if you do a lot of trading, you should ask your broker for a discount on your commission.

Commissions aren't the only way that brokerages make a buck, however. They also charge additional fees for postage and handling, account maintenance, and account inactivity (see Table 13.1). A reputable stockbroker should disclose all fees and commissions that you'll be expected to pay, but if he doesn't, ask him. Here's a sampling of what to expect:

- *Commission.* You'll pay a commission to your broker every time you buy or sell a security. Generally, commissions run higher for more complicated and risky investments. (Why? Because they're harder to sell.) Commissions run about 6% on limited partnerships that invest in speculative ventures, for example, while commissions on actively traded stocks run just 1% to 3%.

> **!** **Two Commissions** If your broker encourages you to trade stocks—rather than holding them for the long term—you'll pay two commissions: one to sell the original stock, another to invest in another stock.

- *Postage and handling.* When you buy or sell a stock, you'll receive a trade confirmation in the mail. Often, the postage and handling fee to mail that notice will be billed to your account.

- *Account management fees.* Some firms charge you an annual fee just to maintain an account. Other firms nail you for an "inactivity" fee if you don't generate at least $100 worth of commissions during the year.

TABLE 13.1   FULL-SERVICE BROKERAGE FIRM COMMISSIONS
AND FEES*
If you bought 500 shares of a $10 stock, you'd pay...

BROKERAGE FIRM	COMMISSION	WIRE TRANSFER	POSTAGE & HANDLING	INACTIVITY FEE
PaineWebber	$177	No	$4.50	No
Smith Barney	$171.95	$25	$4.00	$50**
Merrill Lynch	$164.50	No	$4.85	No
A. G. Edwards	$158	$10	$3.00	No

Annual Brokerage Firm Survey, 1996, National Council of Independent Investors, Washington, D.C.
**After one year with no trades.*

In this lesson, you learned what to expect from a full-service stockbroker. In the next lesson, you will learn what to expect from a discount broker and a deep discount broker.

WORKING WITH A STOCKBROKER— PART 2

In this lesson, you will learn what to expect from a discount broker and a deep discount broker.

If you like to pick your own stocks—and can handle a drop in the market without daily reassurances from your broker that it'll rebound soon—you probably don't need a full-service firm. Go with a *discount broker* instead.

WHAT TO EXPECT FROM A DISCOUNT BROKER

Generally, these no-frills guys can send you (upon request) the very same stock research reports, chock full of analyst's recommendations and opinions, that their full-service brethren gave you. But they won't advise you on which stocks to buy, nor offer much in the way of general investment advice. In return, they charge you less for their services (as their name implies). How much less? About 45% to 70% less than most full-service firms. (See Table 14.1.)

TABLE **14.1**   **HOW LOW CAN THEY GO?**

BROKER	PRICE TO BUY OR SELL	
	100 SHARES AT **$50** PER SHARE	**500 SHARES** AT **$10** PER SHARE
DEEP DISCOUNTERS		
Aufhauser & Co. (800-368-3668)	$27.49	$42.50
Pacific Brokerage Services (800-421-8395)	29.00	29.00
Security Brokerage Services (800-421-8395)	29.00	29.00
Brown & Co. (800-225-6707)	29.00	29.00
Wall Street Equities (800-447-8625)	24.00	24.00
DISCOUNT BROKERS		
Quick & Reilly (800-221-5220)	49.00	60.50
Fidelity Investments (800-544-7272)	54.00	88.50
Charles Schwab (800-435-4000)	55.00	89.00
TYPICAL FULL-SERVICE BROKER	103.00	223.00

*Source: Mercer Discount Brokerage Survey, New York, New York.

The "big three" discount brokers are Quick & Reilly in New York (800-533-8161), Fidelity Investments in Boston (800-544-8666), and Charles Schwab & Co. in San Francisco (800-435-4000). All three companies have offices around the country, which you can visit if you like to make trades in person. Like full-service firms, these three outfits trade every financial product possible and will, when requested, often assign you an individual broker.

To set up an account, call the firm's toll-free telephone number and they'll send you an application. (It's a simple form that asks for your name, address, employer, and bank account number.) Once the broker receives your application, you're ready for action. All you have to do to place a trade is call up your discount broker (just as you would with a full-service broker). You'll then receive a trade confirmation in the mail.

These days, most discount houses run automated service lines that let you place a trade *at any time*. Using your touch-tone phone, you can buy or sell shares seven days a week, 24 hours a day. (Which means that if you're an insomniac—or just a night owl—you can dump those sleepy utility stocks at 2:00 a.m., and buy a more robust stock minutes later.) At many firms you can even get your price quotes read to you over the phone via automated voice mail. Usually, you'll pay even less in commission if you trade through an automatic phone service rather than talk to a live broker.

Most discount shops also have an electronic system for trading over your home computer. Just use your PC to access the dial-up system, such as Fidelity's FundsNetwork, and voilà: You can buy and sell over 2,000 Fidelity and non-Fidelity funds online. How prevalent is this trend? Charles Schwab & Co. offers e.Schwab, a completely electronic version of its discount brokerage service. Interaction with "live" brokers is limited as are visits to local offices. You're charged a flat fee ($29.95) for all stock trades. Another discount firm—aptly named E*Trade—handles electronic stock trades for some 70,000 accounts. When you trade online, brokers will generally cut your commission charge by about 10%.

What to Expect from a Deep Discount Broker

If you really know your way around the stock market, and you want to save even more money on your brokerage commission, try a *deep discount* broker. This bare-bones service will provide the basics—making the trade for you and sending you a monthly statement—at cut-rate fees. In many cases, you'll shell out a whopping 80% less than you'd pay at a full-service firm. (See Table 14.1.)

Don't expect much (if anything) in the way of investment advice, though. You won't get any research on stocks or the market either. And you probably are limited in your product choice. Sure, you can buy stocks, but there are other types of securities, such as municipal bonds, zero coupon bonds, and unit investment trusts, that you probably can't trade through a discount broker.

Then there's the whole "relationship" issue, too. Deep discount firms make their money on *volume,* so investment advice, even a chummy, one-on-one relationship with a customer, is frowned upon. Many times you'll simply talk to a machine. And, if you're lucky enough to talk to a broker on the phone, he probably won't even identify himself by name. (Conversely, you can visit both full-service brokerages and discount brokers in person. There is certainly something to be said for walking into an office and watching a stock market ticker.)

> *tip* **Popular Choice**   As more and more consumers have opted to "do it themselves" over the past several years, deep discounters have grown in number. Today there are about 100. Three examples of deep discount brokerage firms are Jack White & Company in San Diego (800-431-3500), Lombard in San Francisco (800-566-2273), and Brown & Company in Boston (800-822-2021).

The biggest disadvantage of dealing with a deep discount broker, however, may be that your trades aren't always made at the best price (called *execution*). Why? Some investors believe that if their stock orders are "executed" in the principal market in which a stock is traded (such as the New York Stock Exchange), the large volume of buyers and sellers makes it more likely that you'll get a better price. Some stock orders, however, are channeled by discount brokers to "third market," or regional, exchanges. Dealers in these markets pay discounters to bring them their customer's orders, so the discounters may not shop around for the best stock price as they would on a principal market.

To protect yourself, ask your broker if his firm is paid to take orders to particular exchanges. According to a recent Securities and Exchange Commission rule, your broker must indicate this information on your account statements and confirmation slips—upon your request. If your broker *is* working with third market dealers, ask him about the *spread*. More than a quarter of a percentage point difference probably signals that you're not getting the best price. You'd fare better if your stock was traded.

 Spread   The difference between the bid and the asked price of the stock being traded is called the *spread*.

COMMISSIONS AND OTHER FEES

Exactly how cut-rate are these guys? Overall, commissions are definitely much, much lower than at full-service firms. Most discount firms charge a minimum commission of at least $20, but each discounter sets its own pricing schedule. Some firms charge less in commission for large-volume trades; others are cheaper for trades in high-dollar amounts. In addition, many discounters now offer a variety of commission schedules based on whether you talk to a live broker, enter your order by phone or computer, or trade frequently. Commissions vary for the type of product you purchase, too. Actively traded stocks cost less, for example, than more complicated and risky investments.

Even discounters, however, will hit you with some of the following "hidden" costs of trading:

- *Inactivity fees.* You might be penalized if you don't make what the firm considers "enough trades" throughout the year. Expect to be billed an extra $25 to $50 per year.

- *Postage and handling.* At some deep discount firms, every trade will cost you an additional $2 or $3 in handling charges.

- *Dividend reinvestment.* When deep discounters keep your stocks in their "street" names, you often can't participate in the dividend reinvestment program. Some discounters will reinvest the dividends for you—but they'll charge for the service.

- *Margin loans.* If you plan to borrow on margin frequently, the money you save at a discounter could be wiped out in margin loan fees. Some discounters charge up to a full percentage point more for margin loans than their full-service counterparts.

- *Individual retirement account fees.* While a few brokers will waive the start-up and/or annual fees of your IRA account, most don't. Annual fees range from $25 to $40.

- *Other fees.* Some discount brokers charge to transfer your account to another broker (within the same firm) or to register and deliver securities.

---

tip **Discount Pricing Guide** Contact Mercer Inc. (800-582-9854) for discount pricing information. Its annual *Mercer Discount Brokerage Survey* (available for $34.95 plus $3 for shipping) tracks the commissions charged by discount, deep-discount, and full-service brokers.

In this lesson, you learned what to expect from a discount broker and a deep discount broker. In the next lesson, you will learn how to find a broker and how to handle disputes with your broker.

WORKING WITH A STOCKBROKER— PART 3

In this lesson, you will learn how to find a stockbroker, and how to handle disputes with your broker.

FINDING A BROKER

You need a stockbroker that you can trust. Whether you're looking for a discount broker or the full-service variety, ask for recommendations from your family, friends, lawyer, accountant, or colleagues who have income levels and investment objectives similar to your own.

Once you've culled a handful of names, find out whether the recommended brokers and brokerage firms are properly licensed—it's illegal to trade securities *without* a license—by contacting your state securities agency. (Call the North American Securities Administrators Association at 202-737-0900 for the securities agency in your state.)

In addition to being licensed by the state, virtually all stockbrokers and firms must *register* with the National Association of Securities Dealers (NASD). To qualify, brokers must hold a federal license and must pass a Series 7 exam, which tests their knowledge of investments and related issues. Those brokers who wish to trade more exotic investments, such as options, must take additional exams. Continuing education is required. To find out if a broker is a registered agent, call the NASD hotline: 800-289-9999.

Next, check out a broker's employment history and—more important—find out if a broker has committed fraud or any other serious violations by reviewing a broker's Central Registration Depository (CRUD) file. (You can get a CRUD file on a brokerage firm, too.) Most states will relay some of this information over the phone and then follow it up with a copy of the actual CRUD report. Other states require a written request.

Here's what you'll find out in a typical CRUD report:

- Have customers filed complaints against this broker? If so, how many? Are any currently pending?

- Has the broker ever been convicted of fraud?

- What firms has the broker worked for? (You get the broker's employment history for the past ten years.)

- Has the broker been censured, suspended, or disbarred?

- How long has he been registered as a stockbroker?

- Has the firm been involved in a lot of customer suits? Were they ordered to pay damages? How much?

Not Listed? If the state agency can't find a CRUD file for your broker, ask the broker for his "CRUD number." If he doesn't have one, then he may not be a registered agent. You'll probably want to avoid this guy because it's rare for a broker to have a valid license to sell securities and *not* be registered with the NASD.

You can also check out a broker's background with the NASD. Call its toll-free hotline (800-289-9999), which discloses much of the information available on the CRUD. They'll mail or fax you a copy of the CRUD, too, but only if it contains some type of disciplinary information. (If a report contains just employment history, the NASD will read the CRUD over the phone; they won't mail it.) Generally, this CRUD is an abbreviated version of the real thing. It doesn't list pending customer complaints, for instance, or complaints settled through arbitration. A proposal to expand the information available through this hotline is currently in progress.

tip

New Option A *Financial Advisor CheckUp* is now available from the National Council of Individual Investors (800-663-8516). For $39, you'll get what's on the CRUD—plus information from other industries. The logic behind this broader search? This year's broker may have jumped ship from real estate last year and the mortgage business the year before.

WATCH OUT FOR WRONGDOING

Whether you decide on a full-service or a discount broker, you'll need to actively manage your portfolio. It's obvious that you must do this when you choose a discount broker because much of the stock picking and investment planning is up to you. (That's why you pay so much less.) But you should keep an equally close watch if you've hired a full-service broker, too. Huh? Aren't you paying big bucks to let *him* handle matters for you? Not exactly. Only fools delegate complete responsibility of their money and investments to a third party. You should know how and where every single dollar is being invested because, unfortunately, whenever large sums of money trade hands, there's an inevitable temptation for abuse and fraud.

Using a broker's services, you might well lose money in the stock market. You have no protection against bad advice, market slumps, or just plain old incompetence. But you can sometimes force the brokerage firm to make good on your losses if they clearly resulted from a broker's misconduct. The following common problems are *illegal*:

- *Churning.* Brokers earn a commission whenever a security is bought or sold. When unscrupulous brokers make lots of trades—solely to generate sales commissions—it's called "churning."

- *Unauthorized trading.* Your broker executes trades that you didn't order. He may claim that you gave him permission, so be sure to keep records.

- *Unsuitable investments.* If you tell the broker that you want to invest in the stocks of established companies (blue chip stocks, generally), he shouldn't be recommending the latest Internet stock. That investment is

"unsuitable" for your stated investment objectives—
and the broker knows it.

- *Theft.* A broker steals money or stock from your account. This happens more than you might think
because people simply don't read their brokerage
statements. If you had 100 shares of IBM stock last
month, those same 100 shares should still be there
this month (unless *you* sold them).

- *Misrepresentation.* Your broker lies to you, or omits
certain pertinent facts about an investment that he
wants you to buy. He may neglect to tell you that
the company whose stock he's pushing isn't likely to
get FDA approval for its much-hyped new drug, for
instance, which could cause the stock price to drop
dramatically. Or he might tell you that a limited
partnership is not risky. (It is.)

Handling Disputes with Your Broker

If you suspect that your broker is guilty of one or more of the
above abuses, call him immediately and voice your complaint.
Ask him to explain his behavior ("Why did you suggest that I
buy those volatile stocks when you knew that I wanted a
steady income?"), and tell him how you want the problem
corrected. Follow up your conversation with a letter.

If that doesn't bring satisfactory results, complain *in writing* to
the brokerage's branch manager. Include documentation such
as order confirmations and account statements. If *that* doesn't
work, write a similar letter to the firm's compliance officer.

> **! Scare Tactics**   In response to your complaints, some firms may say that if you go to arbitration—and lose—you'll have to pay the broker's legal fees. That never happens. They're just trying to scare you off.

The situation is still unresolved? File a complaint with the state securities commission and the NASD. At this point, you might also want to talk with a lawyer. (Your local bar association can suggest securities or arbitration specialists.) He'll tell you whether your case appears strong or weak, and he'll advise you how to proceed.

> **tip Forget the SEC**   Many consumers automatically assume that they should complain about a broker's misconduct to the Securities and Exchange Commission (SEC). But the SEC can't solve individual cases. Generally, it will only get involved when it's a million-dollar-plus dispute that affects lots of investors. If it's just you and a broker battling over the misuse of $10,000, for example, the SEC will usually refer you to the state securities office.

Chances are, however, that your case won't go to court. Most firms require investors to settle disputes through *arbitration* rather than litigation. Remember that brokerage agreement you signed when you opened your account? Buried in the fine print is a clause that bars you (the investor) from resolving a dispute with a broker in court. Often, in fact, arbitration is your only recourse.

Arbitration   Arbitration is how complaints are typically resolved against brokers. It's a process whereby a conflict is settled outside the official court system. Both sides present their evidence and witnesses (if any) to a presiding arbitrator, who will ultimately grant a decision. Both parties involved must agree in advance to accept the arbitrator's final decision, and, unlike a real court case, appeals are not permitted.

Arbitration panels are sponsored by brokerage-affiliated organizations such as the NASD and the New York Stock Exchange as well as independent entities such as the American Arbitration Association. For details about going to arbitration, contact the NASD (or ask your lawyer). But get moving. Federal law says that claims must be filed within three years of buying a security, or one year of discovering a problem.

tip   **No Representation Needed**   You don't *need* a lawyer to represent you in an arbitration proceeding, but if you're battling a large brokerage firm you can bet that they'll have at least one attorney representing them. If you need to find legal counsel, contact the Public Investors Arbitration Bar Association (800-899-9906). They can refer you to lawyers in your state who can represent you in such disputes.

FIVE *REALLY* GOOD QUESTIONS TO ASK YOUR BROKER

Before you retain a stockbroker's services, ask him or her the following questions:

1. *What's your background?* You want to know about a broker's education and work history. Experience is crucial in the investment business. Ideally, you want someone who's weathered the ups and downs of the market for at least five years.

2. *How much will you and your firm earn on my investments?* A reputable broker should disclose all commissions and fees. Brokers sometimes earn a higher commission, for instance, if they sell individual stocks from the firm's own inventory rather than reselling securities purchased from other brokerages.

3. *How often will we talk to review my portfolio?* If you trade frequently you might be on the phone with your full-service broker on a daily basis. But you should chat every quarter—in person, if possible—to size up your investments and adjust your strategy, if necessary.

4. *How quickly can I get my money out of this investment?* A reputable broker should be able to tell you, *before you invest,* how easy—and how expensive—it is to unload an investment. He should also warn you about any potential tax penalties should you cash an investment in early.

5. *How well have your other clients' investments done?* If the broker won't provide the documentation

himself, ask for three references that you can call. A broker may claim that his client files are confidential—which they are—but he *can* ask his clients' permission to use their names as a reference.

In this lesson, you learned how to find a broker, and how to handle disputes with your broker. In the next lesson, you will learn what to expect from a personal banker.

16

WORKING WITH A BANKER—PART 1

In this lesson, you will learn what to expect from a personal banker.

"LIVE" BANKERS DO EXIST

It's hard to imagine an actual person when you hear the word *banker*. As more and more of us rely on Automatic Teller Machines (ATMs) and online services to make deposits, pay bills, and withdraw cash, we're using a "live" banker less. Plus, one bank after another seems to be merging with its competitor. First it was Chemical and Chase Manhattan. Then it was NationsBank and Bank South, and so on. The reason you don't recognize any faces in that sea of navy suits may well be because they're all *brand new*.

In the past, of course, you knew your banker—personally. Last time you were in the bank, you talked about getting a second mortgage, opening another checking account for your daughter in college—and how the kids were doing in Little League this season. He always took your phone calls. Today, believe it or not, you can still get that very same service from your banker—it's called "personal banking" these days—*if* you know where to look, and who to ask.

WHAT TO EXPECT FROM A PERSONAL BANKER

Banks desperately want your money. They need it to make even *more* money for themselves. Yet competition for your dollars from mutual fund companies, brokerage houses, and competing banks is more fierce than ever. To lure you in—and retain you as a customer—some banks are offering customized service known as *personal banking.*

Here's how it works: In return for your continued business, the bank will cut you a better deal. Let's say that you already have a checking and savings account as well as a home mort-gage loan at one particular bank. You now need a home equity line of credit. Chances are, the bank may pick up the closing costs on that line of credit—and process the papers quickly—because you're a good customer. Or, perhaps you already have a checking account, a certificate of deposit, and a money mar-ket account at the same bank, but you need a second checking account. The bank may throw in overdraft checking privileges as well as a credit card and some travelers checks—gratis.

The more banking that you do at a particular institution, in other words, the more personal attention you'll receive—and the less you'll pay for services. At month's end you may re-ceive a consolidated statement for all of your various accounts. Some surcharges or fees may be reduced, or waived altogether. And in some cases, you may even be able to negotiate a better interest rate on a loan.

Sounds great! Where do you sign up? Unfortunately, that's personal banking's one flaw. It's still sort of a touchy-feely, out-there kind of concept. A handful of banks actually have "personal bankers" on hand. Others assign the duties to a customer service representative. But many leave it up to the branch manager (who already has a lot of other jobs to do). And relatively few actually advertise the service. You may get a letter in the mail if you're already a high-volume customer, but if you have your checking account at Bank 1, your savings at Bank 2, and a mortgage at Bank 3, a personal banker probably won't peddle his service at your doorstep.

Instead, you may have to take the initiative. Visit the branch office of the bank that you're interested in dealing with. Pick up some of the bank's literature on your first visit, and make an appointment with the branch manager or customer service representative, if possible, for a subsequent visit. (An appointment makes you seem like a client, rather than just a window-shopper who wandered in off the street.) Explain what kind of a customer you expect to be. If you do most of your banking by ATM, for instance, find out how much you'll be charged for such usage. Are there surcharges when you use a regional ATM network or a nonproprietary (another bank's) cash machine?

Tell the banker what types of accounts you'd like to open, and how much money you'll be putting in. Talk about the loans you're thinking of taking. (Banks especially love loans; it's how they make their money.) Then ask if the bank offers a personal banking service. If not, ask what the bank can do to accommodate you. (Don't be intimidated by an impatient, brusque, or condescending manner. You're going to give the bank a lot of business. If they don't treat you well, look elsewhere.) Repeat this scene at two other banks. Go with the banker who is the most flexible on the services you use most frequently.

> **tip** **Start Here**   Competition among credit card issu-
> ers is intense, so credit card fees and rates are
> often a good place to start bargaining with your
> bank.

Just what to expect from a personal banker after the initial
sign-up and the subsequent reduction of fees and/or addition
of privileges will vary widely. Most bankers wear several hats.
The same guy who arranges your car loan can probably open
your checking account and set up a CD. But he probably can't
arrange a mortgage. (Generally, mortgages are handled in a
separate division.) That's okay. Your personal banker will simply introduce you to the mortgage man, who will then handle
your loan.

But if your personal banker is any good—and you're truly getting a personal banking service—he should have access to all
of your banking activities, even including those products like
the loan he didn't process himself. That way, when you call
next week or next month—yes, a personal banker should answer your questions over the phone—he can actually tell you
whether there is enough money in your checking account to
transfer funds to pay your mortgage, skip a home-equity payment, and deposit $1,000 into your mutual fund because he's
keeping track of all of those accounts for you.

Personal banking is for everyone (assuming you have a certain
number of accounts, of course, and do a fair amount of business). Don't confuse it with *private banking*, however, a high
level of service that's frequently offered by a bank to its
wealthiest customers. Generally, the bank will offer advice on
financial and estate planning (often in conjunction with its

Trust department) as well as customized products and services. Most customers who warrant this service have assets—excluding their home—worth $1 million or more.

In this lesson, you learned what to expect from a personal banker. In the next lesson, you learn about bank-sponsored mutual funds, and how an asset-management account works.

WORKING WITH A BANKER— PART 2

In this lesson, you will learn about bank-sponsored mutual funds, and how an asset-management account works.

As though investments and banking weren't complicated enough, bankers and brokers have just made the situation a whole lot tougher. Both of these financial specialists are jockeying for an ever larger share of your business. How? By offering you the convenience of handling many of your banking and investing transactions under one roof.

At many banks now, for instance, you can deposit a check into your money market account *and* invest in a mutual fund at the same time. At many brokerage firms, meanwhile, you can now invest in a mutual fund *and* get an interest-bearing checking account. In other words, some banks are now acting like brokerage firms. And many brokerage houses are offering bank-like services.

WHAT TO EXPECT FROM A BANKER WHO ACTS LIKE A BROKER

Since the early '80s, banks have been selling their own versions of mutual funds. Some 3,500 banks now sell what's called *proprietary* funds. Last year, in fact, a third of all new mutual fund sales were made by banks and savings and loans. Managed in-house, these funds are available to anyone—bank customer or not.

Basically, these are the same types of funds—growth, balanced, growth and income, for example—that you'd find at a mutual fund company, except that the bank manages the investment instead of, say, Fidelity or Vanguard. Generally, most of these funds don't have long track records yet either, or exceptionally good returns. (As you might expect from a bank investment, most of them have yielded fairly conservative growth.)

Another type of mutual fund is also available at your local bank. These funds, called *nonproprietary* funds, are *not* home-grown funds managed by your bank. Rather, they're unnamed generic funds created by brokerage firms and sold by banks. Both the banks and the brokerage firms split the fees charged to you.

To date, all bank proprietary mutual funds carry a *load* (or, commission charge). On average, most banks charge a sales load of 4% to 6% on their funds. While that's not more than their mutual fund rivals charge for a similar sales load, these bank funds don't offer any choice but to pay the load. Mutual fund companies, conversely, offer both load funds and no-load funds.

tip   **To Load—Or Not**   A *load* is the cost of advice, basically. If you can pick a fund yourself—without the help of a financial advisor—you shouldn't pay a sales load.

In addition, when you invest in the fund, some banks may also charge you an up-front commission for the salesperson, called a *front-end load*. Others may charge a *back-end load* instead, which is paid when you sell the fund. Banks—and mutual fund companies—can charge up to 8.5% for these loads. (See Table 17.1 for a sampling of the commissions and other fees charged by some bank brokerages.)

Why go to a banker, though, when what you really want is a broker—or simply a mutual fund company? You may feel more comfortable working with your banker—especially if you have a good working relationship with him and if this is your first foray into investing in the stock market. For many consumers, it's natural—and not too anxiety-producing—to move from investing in certificates of deposit at the bank to investing in a bank mutual fund.

The transition isn't as effortless as you might think, however. Your trusted banker can't actually sell you a mutual fund because the Glass-Steagall Act of 1933 prohibits banks from selling investment securities themselves. Banks get around this law, however, by selling you securities through a separate brokerage subsidiary. (This is perfectly legal.) Still, this means that your personal banker can't sell you the goods. He has to introduce you to an investment representative who works for the financial services subsidiary. (Depending on the size of your branch office, an investment representative may be available full-time, or just during selected hours.)

TABLE 17.1   BANK BROKERAGES
If you bought 500 shares of a $10 stock, you'd pay... *

BANK BROKERAGE	COMMISSION	WIRE TRANSFER	POSTAGE & HANDLING	INACTIVITY FEE
Banc One Securities	$88	$10	$2	None
Wachovia Investments	$70	$8.50–$10	None	$30**

BANK BROKERAGE	COMMISSION	WIRE TRANSFER	POSTAGE & HANDLING	INACTIVITY FEE
Barnett Securities	$120	$15	None	None
Nations Securities	$159.21	$20	$2.35	$50**
First Interstate Securities	$58.75	None	$2.50	None

Annual Brokerage Firm Survey, 1996, National Council of Independent Investors.

**After one year with no trades.*

WHAT TO EXPECT FROM A BROKER WHO ACTS LIKE A BANKER

Many brokers are cutting into bankers' traditional turf these days by offering alternatives to your basic checking and savings account. Offered by many full-service and some discount brokerage firms, *asset-management* accounts (or cash-management accounts, as they're sometimes called) combine an interest-paying checking account with a brokerage account and a credit card. With this one account, you can buy and sell stocks, bonds, or some other investment security—plus, write a check to your broker and withdraw cash from an ATM to buy some groceries for dinner.

In addition, an asset-management account acts like a savings account. Any interest or dividends earned on your investment—as well as any proceeds from the sale of your securities—are automatically "swept" into this account daily, where they earn interest at competitive money market rates (about 4.5% currently). That certainly beats dumping your extra cash into a passbook savings account at the bank, earning a mere 2%.

Such privileges are costly, however. The minimum balance requirement for an asset-management account ranges from $5,000 to $25,000; that's much steeper than those for standard checking accounts. ATM transactions are pricier, too. You'll pay as much as $1 for *each* ATM transaction—not counting surcharges—because brokerage houses don't have their own ATM networks. In addition, you'll pay a fee (from $25 to $125 per year) just to maintain the account.

> **!** **ATM Addict**   If you use your ATM card two or three times per week, it's probably cheaper to use a bank than an asset-management account because you're not charged for ATM withdrawals made at a bank's own ATM machine. You're charged for all ATM withdrawals made through an asset-management account.

If you're an active investor, you'll probably like the convenience of this type of account. It's an easy way to keep track of your cash, since one single statement will tell you everything about your investing and banking transactions for the month, such as interest and dividends earned; the purchase and/or sale of securities; purchases made by check or credit card against the account; the current value of your investment.

Are there any risks involved? Your money is certainly as safe as it would be in a bank. All of the assets in the account are insured up to $500,000 (cash, up to $100,000) by the Securities

Investor Protection Corporation. But there's another, rarely talked about, danger. Asset-management accounts are margin accounts, too. That means you can borrow against your securities—generally up to 50% of the value of your stock. Some investors—especially novice investors—borrow against their account without realizing the terms of this debt. Unlike bank loans, these loans can be called in for payment at any time. If you don't have the cash, you'll have to sell your securities and use the money to repay the debt.

If you're interested in setting up an asset-management account—and you have enough money to satisfy the minimum-balance requirements and cover the fees—ask your broker. Or contact one of these brokerage firms:

- *Merrill Lynch* (800-262-4636). Merrill Lynch created the "sweep-account" market with its Cash Management Account. Today, the firm has 1.9 million different accounts.

- *Charles Schwab* (800-435-4000). Charles Schwab now has more than 500,000 accounts.

In this final lesson, you learned about bank-sponsored mutual funds, and how an asset-management account works.

Over the course of this book, you learned what to expect from a variety of financial advisors. You learned about the fees charged and the qualifications and licensing required by each professional group. You also learned how to find such advisors and when you would benefit most from such professional advice. Hopefully, this information will help you select a trusted advisor or two, whose services you'll retain for all your financial needs.

State Bar Associations

State bar associations are excellent resources for consumers. They can provide information about lawyer referrals, *pro bono* services, lawyer discipline, and other topics. Below is a complete listing of state bars.

Alabama State Bar
P.O. Box 671
Montgomery, AL 36101
334-269-1515

Alaska Bar Association
P.O. Box 100279
Anchorage, AK 99510
907-272-7469

State Bar of Arizona
111 W. Monroe
Suite 1800
Phoenix, AZ 85003
602-252-4804

Arkansas Bar Association
400 W. Markham
Little Rock, AR 72201
501-375-4605

State Bar of California
555 Franklin Street
San Francisco, CA 94102
415-561-8200

Colorado Bar Association
1900 Grant Street
9th floor
Denver, CO 80203
303-860-1115

Connecticut Bar Association
101 Corporate Place
Rocky Hill, CT 06067
860-721-0025

Delaware State Bar Association
1201 Orange Street
Suite 1100
Wilmington, DE 19801
302-658-5279

Bar Association of the District
of Columbia
1819 H St., NW
12th Floor
Washington, DC 20006
202-223-6600

District of Columbia Bar
1250 H St., NW
6th Floor
Washington, DC 20005
202-737-4700

Florida Bar
650 Apalachee Parkway
Tallahassee, FL 32399-2300
904-561-5600

State Bar of Georgia
800 The Hurt Bldg.
50 Hurt Plaza
Atlanta, GA 30303
404-527-8700

Hawaii State Bar Association
1136 Union Mall
Penthouse 1
Honolulu, HI 96813
808-537-1868

Idaho State Bar
P.O. Box 895
Boise, ID 83701
208-334-4500

Illinois State Bar Association
424 S. Second St.
Springfield, IL 62701
217-525-1760

Indiana State Bar Association
230 E. Ohio Street, 4th Fl.
Indianapolis, IN 46204
317-639-5465

Iowa State Bar Association
521 E. Locust
Des Moines, IA 50309
515-243-3179

Kansas Bar Association
1200 SW Harrison
P.O. Box 1037
Topeka, KS 66601-1037
913-234-5696

Kentucky Bar Association
514 West Main Street
Frankfort, KY 40601-1883
502-564-3795

Louisiana State Bar Association
601 St. Charles Ave.
New Orleans, LA 70130
504-566-1600

Maine State Bar Association
P.O. Box 788
Augusta, ME 04332-0788
207-622-7523

Maryland State Bar Association
520 W. Fayette St.
Baltimore, MD 21201
410-685-7878

Massachusetts Bar Association
20 West St.
Boston, MA 02111
617-542-3602

State Bar of Michigan
306 Townsend St.
Lansing, MI 48933-2083
517-372-9030

Minnesota State Bar
Association
514 Nicollet Mall
Suite 300
Minneapolis, MN 55402
612-333-1183

Mississippi Bar
P.O. Box 2168
Jackson, MS 39225-2168
601-948-4471

Missouri Bar
P.O. Box 119
Jefferson City, MO 65102
573-635-4128

State Bar of Montana
P.O. Box 577
Helena, MT 59624
406-442-7660

Nebraska State Bar
Association
635 S. 14th St.
Lincoln, NE 68508
402-475-7091

State Bar of Nevada
201 Las Vegas Blvd. S.
Suite 200
Las Vegas, NV 89101
702-382-2200

New Hampshire Bar
Association
112 Pleasant St.
Concord, NH 03301
603-224-6942

New Jersey State Bar
Association
New Jersey Law Center
One Constitution Square
New Brunswick, NJ 08901-1500
908-249-5000

State Bar of New Mexico
5121 Masthead NE
Albuquerque, NM 87109
505-797-6000

New York State Bar Association
One Elk St.
Albany, NY 12207
518-463-3200

North Carolina State Bar
200 Fayetteville Street Mall
Raleigh, NC 27601
919-828-4620

North Carolina Bar Association
P.O. Box 3688
Raleigh, NC 27519
919-677-0561

State Bar Association of North
Dakota
P.O. Box 2136
Bismarck, ND 58502
701-255-1404

Ohio State Bar Association
P.O. Box 16562
Columbus, OH 43216-6562
614-487-2050

Oklahoma Bar Association
P.O. Box 53036
Oklahoma City, OK 73152
405-524-2365

Oregon State Bar
P.O. Box 1689
Lake Oswego, OR 97035
503-620-0222

Pennsylvania Bar Association
P.O. Box 186
Harrisburg, PA 17108
717-238-6715

Puerto Rico Bar Association
P.O. Box 1900
San Juan, PR 00903
809-721-3358

Rhode Island Bar Association
115 Cedar Street
Providence, RI 02903
401-421-5740

South Carolina Bar
P.O. Box 608
Columbia, SC 29202
803-799-6653

State Bar of South Dakota
222 E. Capitol Avenue
Pierre, SD 57501
605-224-7554

Tennessee Bar Association
3622 West End Avenue
Nashville, TN 37205
615-383-7421

State Bar of Texas
P.O. Box 12487
Austin, TX 78711
512-463-1463

Utah State Bar
645 S. 200 East
Salt Lake City, UT 84111
801-531-9077

Vermont Bar Association
P.O. Box 100
Montpelier, VT 05601
802-223-2020

Virginia State Bar
707 E. Main Street
Suite 1500
Richmond, VA 23219-2803
804-775-0500

Virginia Bar Association
701 E. Franklin St.
Suite 1120
Richmond, VA 23219
804-644-0041

Virgin Islands Bar Association
P.O. Box 4108
Christiansted, St. Croix 00822
809-778-7497

Washington State Bar
  Association
2101 Fourth Ave.
Seattle, WA 98121
206-727-8200

West Virginia State Bar
2006 Kanawha Boulevard East
Charleston, WV 25311-2204
304-558-2456

State Bar of Wisconsin
402 W. Wilson
Madison, WI 53703
608-257-3838

Wyoming State Bar
P.O. Box 109
Cheyenne, WY 82003
307-632-9061

Source: American Bar Association, Public Education Division.

INDEX